A Rainbow Book

BOATER
101

A FULL-REFERENCE GUIDE TO BOATING BASICS

Marine University

Rainbow Books, Inc.
FLORIDA

Library of Congress Cataloging-in-Publication Data

Marine University.
   Boater 101 : a full-reference guide to boating basics / by Marine University.
     p. cm.
   Includes index.
   ISBN 1-56825-111-4 (trade softcover : alk. paper)
   1. Boats and boating—Handbooks, manuals, etc. I. Title.
   GV775.M37 2007
   797.1—dc22

2006037469

Boater101: A Full-Reference Guide to Boating Basics
© 2007 by Marine University
www.MarineUniversity.org • www.Boater101.com

ISBN-10: 1-56825-111-4
ISBN-13: 978-1-56825-111-0

Published by
Rainbow Books, Inc.
P. O. Box 430
Highland City, FL 33846-0430

Editorial Offices and Wholesale/Distributor Orders
Telephone: (863) 648-4420
Email: RBIbooks@aol.com
www.RainbowBooksInc.com

Individuals' Orders
Toll-free Telephone (800) 431-1579 • www.AllBookStores.com

The paper used in this publication meets the minimum requirements of the American National Standard for Information Sciences—Permanence of Paper for Printed Library Materials, ANSI Z39.48-1984.

First Edition 2007
12 11 10 09 08 07   7 6 5 4 3 2 1

Printed in the United States of America.

Welcome to the Boater101 Program!

Congratulations! You have just taken the first step to boating safely by participating in the *BOATER101* program. *BOATER101* is a fun, informative way to learn about boating safety and environmental awareness. This program was developed in 1993 by Marine University, a non-profit organization, through collaboration with marine industry members. The goal of this program is to create an educational experience that the participants will use throughout their lives.

To become a certified boater, you must complete the following steps:

1. Familiarize yourself with the federal boating safety information included in the Boater101 Manual.

2. Visit the Boater101 web site to review state-specific information for your state. Each state has boating laws in addition to the federal regulations discussed in this manual that are unique. You must familiarize yourself with your state's regulations to ensure that you are following all the appropriate laws.

3. Finish the course by either taking an online exam or classroom course. During these courses, you will be able to learn from supplemental materials including color navigation graphics. The availability of the online exam or classroom course is dependent on state requirements. You will be directed to the appropriate venue once you register online.

We wish to express our gratitude to our sponsors who have made Boater101 possible: **Brunswick, Formula, Genmar, INAMAR, KeyBank, Marine Industries Association of South Florida, National Marine Manufacturers Association, OMC Foundation** and **Volvo Penta**.

We hope you enjoy the program!

Course approved by the National Association of State Boating Law Administrators and recognized by the U.S. Coast Guard as acceptable to the Recreational Boating Safety Program.

info@marineuniversity.org • www.marineuniversity.org

CONTENTS

CONTENTS

CONTENTS

CHAPTER 1

INTRODUCTION TO BOATING

Boating Safety Education

At the current time, federal law does not require boaters to take a boating safety course. Most states, however, require that boaters under a certain age pass a boating safety course to be allowed to operate a boat. In addition to a basic boating safety course, new boaters should continue their education by taking a course that focuses on boat handling and operation. It is also important that boaters are aware that state boating safety laws are updated on an annual basis. Boaters are responsible for staying informed of any changes to state boating safety requirements. Consult your specific state laws for more information or visit our website: www.boater101.com.

CHAPTER 1 - INTRODUCTION TO BOATING

Boat Terminology

The first step in becoming a safe boater is to familiarize yourself with basic boating terminology. Boating language originates from many places, including ancient Greece, the Roman Empire, Scandinavia and England. For instance, the word starboard comes from the Norwegian language. The rudder, or stjorn, pronounced "starn," is located on the right side of the boat. Thus, the side of the boat became known as starn board, hence the name starboard. The word port has also evolved in a similar manner. When a vessel would dock, it would always dock with the left side of the boat towards the wharf. Vessels would load cargo through port openings in their sides; hence, the left side became known as the port side.

For the purposes of understanding the Navigational Rules of the Road that will be described later in this manual, you should understand that the word vessel is used indiscriminately to describe every type of watercraft that could be used as a means of transportation on the water, including seaplanes. The term motorized vessel or powerboat is used to describe any vessel that is mechanically powered by an engine. Sailboats refer only to vessels that are being operated by sail only. Since many sailboats are equipped with engines, they are considered powerboats when their engines are in use, even if their sails are up. The term underway is used to describe any vessel that is not anchored, moored or aground. The keel of a boat is located on the centerline on the bottom of a boat and runs from the front to the back of the boat. The bilge is a compartment, located underneath the floorboards inside the hull near the bottom of the boat. Additional boating terms are listed below and correlate with the numbers indicated on the associated graphics.

CHAPTER 1 - INTRODUCTION TO BOATING

1. Port: The left side of the boat as you face forward

2. Starboard: The right side of the boat as you face forward.

3. Helm: Where the boat operator sits (or stands); throttle, shift and steering controls are located at the helm

4. Throttle: Controls engine speed

5. Beam: The width of a boat at its widest point

6. Hull: The basic "shell" of the boat

7. Transom: The vertical part of the stern; between the hull sides

8. Bow: The front of the boat.

9. Forward: Towards the bow (or front) of the boat

10. Aft: Towards the stern (or back of the boat)

11. Stern: The back of a boat

12. Wake: The path left by a moving boat in water; a wave

13. Gunwale: The top of the boat's sides

14. Waterline: Where the water meets the sides (and bow/stern) of the boat

15. Freeboard: How high the boat's sides are; measured from the waterline to the top of the gunwale

16. Draft: How deep the boat sits in the water; measured from the waterline to the lowest part of the bottom of the boat

Boat Designs

Types of Boats

It's a given – boats float and are propelled in three different ways: manually by oars or paddles, mechanically by an engine or naturally through wind and sail. There are also different types of boats for different types of activities. Some of these activities might include fishing, water skiing, cruising or wind surfing. A boat's construction plays a major role in determining which type of boat you select for your favorite activity.

Basic Hull Designs

The shell of the boat is called the hull, and there are two basic hull designs, planing and displacement. Each hull acts in a similar manner when the boat is idling or moving slowly; however, the hulls react differently when speed is increased.

Planing Hulls

When a boat increases its speed, the bow lifts out of the water and skims the surface, keeping much of the hull dry and out of the water. These types of boats tend to travel at high speeds. If the water surface is not calm, a planing hull will bounce on top of the water and create a very choppy ride.

Displacement Hulls

Displacement hulls allow boats to ride very comfortably in water but prevent them from going very fast. The water surrounding the boat is displaced to allow the hull to plow through the water. This type of boat gets a large part of its hull wet as it moves through the water.

Hull Shapes

Understanding the boat's hull is an important factor in boating safety. We are going to discuss the most common types of boat hulls, their designs and their uses. Boats and their functions are extremely similar to cars and their uses. What type of car would you use to haul hay to a dusty farm, a bright shiny red Corvette or a truck? Would you drive a convertible in the rain? Would you feel safe crossing the Atlantic or Pacific Ocean in a canoe?

Boats can have monohulls or multihulls. A monohull is a boat, which makes a single "footprint" in the water when loaded to its rated capacity. Multihulls are boats that have more than one hull. For example, a catamaran, trimaran or a pontoon boat is not a monohull boat but rather a multihull boat.

Round Bottom Boat

Round bottom boats maneuver easily through the water, but can be unstable when weight is not evenly distributed. These boats tend to tip and roll if not operated properly.

Flat Bottom Boats

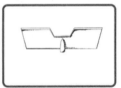

Flat bottom boats operate most efficiently on calm waters. They plane easily, and many boaters enjoy their simple handling. This type of boat is not very stable when operated at high speeds, and will pound on the water's surface for an uncomfortable ride.

Vee Bottom Boats

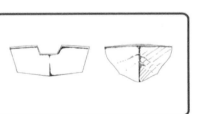

Vee and deep vee bottom boats provide a smoother ride in choppy water when compared to flat and round bottom boats. A deep vee bottom boat planes well and requires additional horsepower to maintain speed, producing a more comfortable ride.

Multihull Boat

Multihull boats provide more stability and speed because of their wide beam. They also provide less resistance while moving through the water. Multi-hulls are boats that have more than one hull. For example, a catamaran, trimaran or a

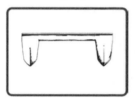

pontoon boat is not a monohull boat but rather a multihull boat.

Boat Classifications

When operating your boat, there are certain rules and regulations that must be followed. Both federal and state boating agencies regulate vessel operation.

Your boat may fall under one of six length classifications, determining if it needs to be registered and numbered, or if a license needs to be obtained. The length of the vessel is determined by measuring from one end of the vessel to the other end, along the centerline. In measuring length, do not include motors, brackets, fittings or other apparatuses attached to the outside of the boat. The length of a vessel dictates the equipment required onboard and the regulations that are applied.

UNDER 16 FT

16 TO LESS THAN 26 FT

26 TO LESS THAN 40 FT

40 TO LESS THAN 65 FT

65 TO LESS THAN 110 FT

GREATER THAN 110 FT

Types of Motors

Outboard Engines

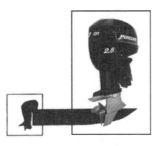

An outboard engine is mounted to the transom of the boat, outside of the hull. Outboards are common on boats from 12 to 40 feet in length. They consist of four main components:

1. Engine: The engine (or power head) is located at the top of the outboard.

2. Mid-section: The mid-section (or drive shaft housing) is situated vertically, just beneath the engine.

3. Gear case: The gear case (or lower unit) is at the bottom of the outboard. The gear case houses the forward and reverse gears; it also has a rudder-type feature called a "skeg" that also protects the propeller from damage.

4. Propeller: The propeller is fastened to the rear of the gear case. The propeller transmits the power of the engine to the water.

There are two main types of outboard engines: Two cycle (or two-stroke) and four cycle (or four-stroke). Two-stroke engines mix lubricating oil with gasoline. In recent years, a variety of computerized direct fuel injection systems have made two-stroke outboards much more efficient and environmentally friendly than in the past. Typically, two-stroke outboards weigh less than four-stroke outboards and still have comparable horsepower. Four-stroke engines do not mix gas and oil. These engines are very similar to automobile engines and are gaining popularity for their smooth/quiet running quality, fuel efficiency and low emissions. There are several benefits to outboard motors. For example, outboard motors have an excellent power to weight ratio, they are easy to service and replace and do not take up space in the boat. A disadvantage of outboard motors, however, is that they are generally more limited in maximum practical power output when compared with a stern drive. This means that to power a large boat with, for example, 800 horsepower, it may require three outboard motors versus two stern drive engines.

Inboard Engines

An inboard engine is located inside the hull of the boat. Power from the engine is transmitted to the propeller via a shaft that runs from the engine, through the bottom of the boat to the prop. Beneath the boat, a rudder is mounted aft of the propeller. The advantage of an inboard engine is that they do not have a complicated lower unit. The disadvantages of an inboard engine are that in a single-engine installation, they require greater skill to maneuver, particularly in reverse, and can take up a significant amount of space inside the boat. V-drive inboards can be packaged at the aft-most portion of the boat to free up cockpit space, but the more rearward center of gravity can hinder the quick planning advantages of the inboard design.

Inboard/Outboard (I/O) or Stern Drive Engines

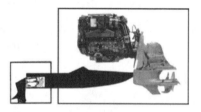

Stern drive engines combine features from both inboard and outboard engines. Like an inboard engine, a stern drive engine has the engine mounted inside the boat's hull. Like an outboard engine, the stern drive engine has the propulsion unit, also known as the outdrive, located outside the stern on the transom. The four main advantages of the stern drive engine are that they are more efficient and quieter than outboards, are available at significantly higher horsepower levels and they tend to be more durable. However, the disadvantages to stern drive engines are that they take up space inside the boat, tend to be heavier than comparable outboard power and because of their extra weight can add draft to smaller boats.

Jet Engines

Boats such as Personal Watercraft (PWC) are powered by an inboard engine and propelled through the water by the action of a jet pump.

The jet pump draws in water then forces it out through the steerable nozzle that controls the direction of the boat. The main advantages of a jet boat are that they 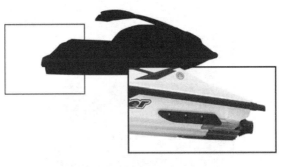 are highly maneuverable, responsive and can be operated in shallow waters. The disadvantages of a jet boat are that the jet pump can easily clog and they require power to turn.

Water Activities

Water Skiing and Other Aquaplaning Devices

Water skiing, tubing or use of another aquaplaning device is a great way to spend a day on the water. Many states have different regulations concerning towing an aquaplaning device. A responsible tow team should include an operator, observer  (which is required in many states) and the person being towed. Many states have minimum age requirements for observers and may require them to use a Red or Orange ski flag at least 12 by 12 inches in size to indicate when a person is in the water. In addition, most states have regulations that only allow towing during daylight or near daylight hours. It is the responsibility of the operator of the vessel to make sure all state regulations are followed. No one may ski or use another aquaplaning device while impaired by alcohol or other drugs. While water skiing or participating in any other activity on a boat, the water skier must wear a Type I, II, III or V personal flotation device and, of course, a PFD must be available to each person onboard.

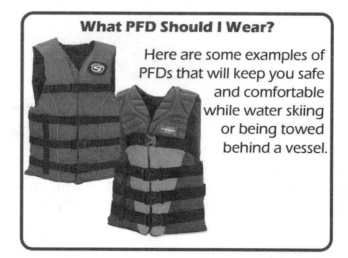

What PFD Should I Wear?

Here are some examples of PFDs that will keep you safe and comfortable while water skiing or being towed behind a vessel.

Skier Hand Signals

(Provided by the American Water Ski Association)

1. Speed-Up: The "thumbs-up" gesture indicates that the skier would like the speed increased.

2. Slow Down: The "thumbs-down" gesture indicates that the skier would like the speed decreased.

3. O.K.: If the newly set speed or boat path is good, then the skier may use the O.K. signal.

4. Turn: When either the skier or the driver wants the boat turned, a circle motion with the arm over the head with one finger in the air is used. Pointing in the direction of the turn usually follows this signal.

5. Back to the Dock: A pat on the head indicates that the skier would like to return to the dock.

6. Cut Motor/Stop: A slashing motion with the hand across the neck indicates the boat is to stop immediately. The skier, driver or observer can use this signal.

7. I'm O.K. (after a fall): This important signal indicates that a skier is O.K. after a fall. It consists of both hands clasped over the head. As a coach, insist upon seeing it every time.

When water skiing, the operator of the boat should start at slow speed. After making sure the area ahead is clear, the skier is ready and the towrope is tight, the operator then gives the boat enough power to raise the skier. The skier will provide the operator with hand signals indicating his or her intent for speed and direction. In order to avoid a risk of collision, the operator should not pull the skier close to a fixed object or another vessel.

When the skier falls, the skier either holds both hands clasped over his/her head or holds up a ski to alert the boat operator. The operator slowly circles around, so the towline will be in a position to be used for getting up again. If the skier decides to board the boat, the motor should be stopped to minimize the risk of injury by propeller strike, and the skier should be assisted onboard from the stern.

When boating in the vicinity of another boat that is towing a person on skis or other aquaplaning device, you should maintain a safe distance away from the other vessel. Keep a lookout for fallen skiers or other persons in the water. Do not navigate close to the stern of a  towing vessel, even if both vessels are operating at idle or slow speed, as there may be a towline in the water that could get caught in your propeller.

CHAPTER 1 - INTRODUCTION TO BOATING

Fishing

One of the most popular recreational water sports is fishing. As a boat operator, you must be aware of fishermen (anglers) within your area. Keep in mind that fishing lines are difficult to see, so be sure to give anglers plenty of room. It is a good idea to slow down as you approach fishing boats to prevent their vessel from being pounded or even swamped by your wake. It is important to be courteous to others, who are enjoying the same body of water as you and your vessel.

What PFD Should I Wear?

Here are some examples of PFDs that will keep you safe and comfortable while fishing.

If you decide to use your boat for fishing, be sure you are prepared. You should always wear a PFD and follow all federal and state navigational rules that are applicable to recreational boats. Before you go out on the boat, be aware of your state's fishing regulations. In many states, fish are protected by seasons and catch limits, and a permit is required before you begin your day out on the water. If a marine patrol officer stops you, you will be required to show him a fishing license for each angler on the boat.

The following table is an example of a catch limit table:

Species	Seasons	Min. Size	Daily Possesion Limit
Largemouth Bass	6/15 - 12/31	14"	5 in any combination but no more than 2 Northern Pike
Smallmouth Bass	5/25 - 12/31	14"	
Walleye	5/15 - 2/13	15"	
Sauger	4/27 - 3/15	15"	
Northern Pike	Open All Year	24"	
Flathead Catfish	Open All Year	15"	

When fishing, avoid anchoring or drifting across shipping or other busy channels. Never moor to buoys or other navigational aids. Since many fishing boats are smaller vessels, you should understand the safety concerns associated with small boats such as the risk of capsizing or swamping. Never exceed the listed capacities on the Capacity Plate. To prevent yourself and others from falling overboard, do not lean over the side of the boat to land your catch or stand up quickly. Knowing these safety tips and requirements will ensure that you have an enjoyable time on the water.

Hunting

Hunting may also involve the use of small boats. It is again important for hunters to wear a PFD and follow all federal and state navigational rules that are applicable to recreational boats. You should never stand in your boat while hunting as gun recoil can cause you to lose your balance. It is especially important not to fire a shot or release an arrow until the boat is stopped. Remaining seated or kneeling in your vessel and distributing your gear evenly will decrease the likelihood of you capsizing or swamping your boat. If you encounter rough weather, keep a low center of gravity.

Like fishing, many states stipulate which animals are hunted, determine the seasons and limit the number of catch. It is also important to obtain the proper permits and licenses required by your state's regulations before going out on your boat.

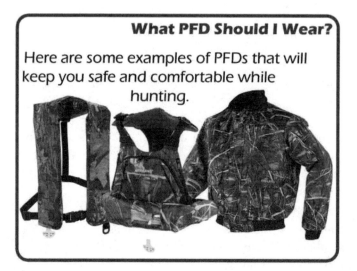

What PFD Should I Wear?

Here are some examples of PFDs that will keep you safe and comfortable while hunting.

Diving

Diving is a popular water sport and most divers utilize the same bodies of water as recreational boaters. Boat operators must be aware of divers in their area.

Divers are required in many states to use either an alpha or "A" flag, which signals that the vessel is restricted in its ability to maneuver while engaged in diving operations or a more common recreational red "Divers Down" flag, which indicates that SCUBA or snorkel divers are in the area. This flag can be either flown from the boat that is mothering the SCUBA or snorkel divers or carried with the divers themselves on a buoy.

WHITE AND BLUE
"A" FLAG

RED AND WHITE
DIVERS DOWN FLAG

If you see one of these flags, be sure to stay the required distance away as determined by your state's laws. Many states require a distance of at least 100 feet between the flag and your vessel. In bays and open water, stay 300 feet away. Also keep a lookout for air bubbles breaking the surface, which can indicate a diver that has accidentally drifted outside of the diving area.

As a snorkel or SCUBA diver, you should be aware of your surroundings. Avoid diving in constrained areas such as inlets or canals where boats could have difficulty avoiding you. If you are SCUBA diving, make sure that you have taken the appropriate courses to receive your certification. When you go out on a boat to dive, make sure you have chosen a vessel appropriate to your activity. Do not overload your boat with gear and make sure that it is stable. It is a good idea to always have one person remain on the boat while the other divers are in the water so that he or she can act as a lookout in case a problem should arise.

SCUBA and snorkel divers should also practice proper resource friendly diving techniques in order to preserve the environment. Many of the resources that attract divers such as coral reefs are threatened and experiencing dramatic declines. To ensure the availability of these resources in the future divers should be careful not to negatively impact the environment.

Paddle Boats

Canoe, kayaks and rafts offer some of the most enjoyable boating experiences in both inland and coastal waters. Using one of these vessels, however, requires caution. You must be aware of the safety concerns of operating a manually propelled vessel. Observe the tips discussed in the following sections to ensure a safe and fun experience when paddling.

CHAPTER 1 - INTRODUCTION TO BOATING

Be prepared to enter the water.

- Paddle boats such as canoes and kayaks capsize easily. You should always wear a personal flotation device.

- Avoid the use of alcohol. If you capsize, you are better prepared to deal with an emergency situation if you maintain clear judgment.

- Know how to swim and how to get out of the water or a current in the event of capsizing.

  o If you capsize in a river, float on the upstream side of the boat. This will prevent you from being pinned between your boat and another object as you float downstream.

  o Do not try to stand up in a river or swift moving current and walk to the shore. Float on your back with your feet downstream until you reach an area where the current is moving slowly enough for you to comfortably swim ashore.

Minimize the possibility of capsizing.

- Avoid standing up or moving about in a canoe or kayak.

  o If you must move around, maintain three points of contact. For example, as you lift a foot to step forward, you should hold onto the boat with both hands. If both feet are firmly placed on the floor of the boat, move one hand at a time.

- Load the boat properly, making sure all weight is evenly distributed. Heavier items should be stowed as low and close to the boat's centerline as possible. Do not overload your boat.

- Do not lean over the sides of the boat. Keep your shoulders between the boat's sides.

o If you must retrieve something in the water, use your paddle to pull it close to the side of the boat before reaching to pick it up.

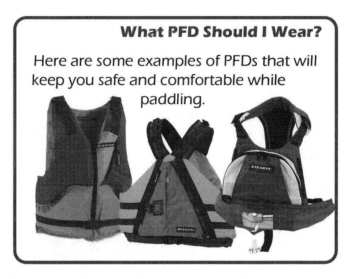

What PFD Should I Wear?

Here are some examples of PFDs that will keep you safe and comfortable while paddling.

Think safety first.

- Take hands-on training with a qualified instructor. Learn the basics of the paddle boat activity you are interested in. Practice the different type of paddle strokes until you can easily maneuver your boat. White water kayakers should learn to right themselves when they roll over. Familiarize yourself with safety techniques and how to enter and exit the water.

- Make sure the water conditions are not more demanding than your skill level. This is especially important when you are white water rafting or operating in an area with strong waves or current.

- Never paddle alone. Always paddle with another boat so that you will be able to assist each other in the event of an emergency.

- Establish and keep, a general route and timetable.

- Pay attention to the weather. Since manually propelled vessels are much slower than motor boats, it is even more important that you monitor the weather and give yourself an ample amount of time to reach a safe place before a storm hits or unfavorable conditions appear.

- Be aware that it may be difficult for other boaters to spot you. If you are in a lake, stay relatively close to shore.

- During cold weather, take the proper precautions to avoid hypothermia (See Chapter 4 for more information on hypothermia).

Personal Watercraft

© 2005 Bombardier Recreational Products Inc. (BRP)

Personal watercraft (PWC) make up a large segment of the United States watercraft industry. PWC have to follow the same navigational rules as other powerboats. Because of their size, maneuverability and speed, PWC appear to be easy to operate. By applying what you will learn concerning proper boat, required safety equipment, knowledge of navigational rules, environmental laws and no-wake zones, you will be on your way to becoming a responsible PWC operator. Please be aware that every person who operates a PWC is responsible for being educated about safe operation.

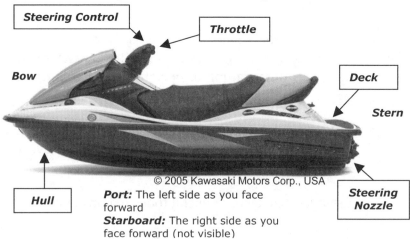

Steering Control

Throttle

Bow

Deck

Stern

© 2005 Kawasaki Motors Corp., USA

Hull

Port: The left side as you face forward
Starboard: The right side as you face forward (not visible)

Steering Nozzle

CHAPTER 1 - INTRODUCTION TO BOATING

Engine Mechanics

PWC are engineered differently than most boats. Since they are a jet boat, the water being forced out through the steerable nozzle controls the direction of the boat. If you release the throttle or shut-off the ignition, you may lose all steering control. When trying to avoid a collision, your first reaction will be to let go of the throttle. Remember that you must always have some thrust or throttle in order to steer a PWC, so you should learn how to make both high-speed and low-speed maneuvers with the throttle. PWC are now required to have a form of "off-throttle" steering, which will help in some situations but it is best to learn to steer using the throttle.

Steering a PWC

There are three ways to steer a PWC. These include using the handlebars, your body movement and a combination of both the handlebars and body movement. The handlebars are connected to the steerable exhaust nozzle allowing you to change direction. The nozzle will turn in the same direction as the handlebars causing the thrust of the water jet to push the PWC in the desired direction. PWC can also be steered using body movement. Similar to a motorcycle, you can control your direction by shifting your body weight and leaning in the desired direction. The shift in weight causes the stern of the vessel to move in the opposite direction and turn the PWC as desired.

Be aware, however, the body movement technique is only effective at high speeds. Finally, you can use both handlebars and body movement combined. This combination will allow you to make sharp and quick turns in shorter distances. Caution should be used, however, when using both the handlebars and your body weight to control steering since if you complete the turns too quickly, you can lose control and be thrown from the vessel.

Capsizing and Reboarding

PWC are also different from other vessels in that they are built to capsize. If you capsize your PWC, most manufacturers have placed a decal on the back of the vessel indicating which way to roll the PWC into an upright position. You will typically reboard a PWC behind the craft, using your legs and a handle on the back of the seat to pull yourself up. Some PWC even have reboarding ladders to make the process easier. It is a good idea to practice reboarding in shallow water, so if you fall off in deep water, it will not be as difficult to reboard.

Most PWC are equipped with a lanyard or cut-off switch that you should attach to your PFD, clothing or your wrist. If you happen to fall off the PWC, this will kill the engine, and allow you to swim safely to the PWC. Always operate a PWC within the capacity limits stated by the manufacturer. Do not overload your PWC.

As indicated in the picture, newer PWC are now equipped with capacity plate stickers that are usually located toward the stern of the vessel on either side. If there is not a capacity plate sticker on the PWC, loading capacities can be found in the PWC's operator manual.

Monitoring Fuel Useage

When operating a PWC, boaters should pay attention to their fuel usage. Most PWC are equipped with separate fuel tanks designated as "main" and "reserve". A fuel selector switch either on the side of the vessel or on the dashboard allows you to switch between the two tanks. For general operation, you should keep the selector switch on the "main" tank since the "reserve" tank only holds about one gallon of fuel. If you run low on fuel and have to switch to the "reserve" tank, you should head straight to shore. Once you re-fuel the vessel, be sure to change the selector switch back to the "main" tank. You should monitor your fuel usage and plan on using one-third of your fuel tank when you are going out, one-third to return and one-third as a reserve that can be used for unexpected circumstances.

Safety Equipment

PWC must also carry safety equipment as required for other vessels; however, these requirements are slightly modified. For example, PWC operators and passengers must wear a USCG-approved PFD at all times. This PFD must be approved for use on a PWC and cannot be an inflatable type. Manufacturers do not equip PWC with navigation lights; therefore, they are not intended for use from sunset to sunrise or in periods of reduced visibility. Check your state's regulations for information on the appropriate time and place for PWC operation. Be aware that even if you add navigation lights to your PWC, in most states they are still restricted from being operated from sunset to sunrise. PWC operators must also carry a USCG-approved Type B fire extinguisher onboard their vessel. It is also recommended that PWC operators and passengers wear appropriate protective clothing such as eye protection, soft-soled shoes and a wet suit. PWC operators should always wear the lanyard or cut-off switch when operating their vessel as previously described in the Capsizing and Reboarding section. Individual states may also have additional equipment requirements for PWC.

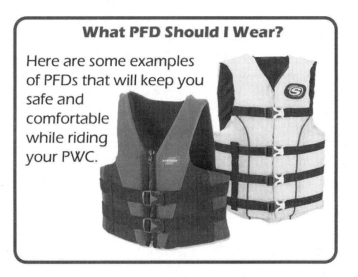

What PFD Should I Wear?

Here are some examples of PFDs that will keep you safe and comfortable while riding your PWC.

CHAPTER 1 - INTRODUCTION TO BOATING

PWC Usage

As a PWC operator, you are primarily responsible for preventing a PWC accident. You should also be aware that the use of PWC is not appropriate in all waters. For example, some National Parks and states restrict the use of PWC on certain water bodies. Since each state varies in its PWC regulations and age restrictions, be sure to familiarize yourself with your state's PWC regulations prior to operation.

Tips for Safe and Courteous PWC operation

- Follow the manufacturer's recommendations on:

    o Loading capacities

    o Reboarding your PWC

    o Operation

- Remember that you are responsible for yourself, your passengers and any damage your PWC or your wake may cause.

- Move around the waterways rather than staying in one location. This will lessen the noise associated with the operation of your PWC and be less disruptive to your neighbors. In addition, some states require that boats be equipped with effective muffling devices to minimize noise pollution. Be sure to check with your local state agency so that you will be in compliance with your state's regulations.

Safe operation includes taking all necessary precautions and actions to avoid accidents, avoiding others in the water and preventing negative impacts to the environment.

- When overtaking another personal watercraft, stay well clear of the other craft and refrain from making sudden or erratic moves. If you are being overtaken, maintain your speed and course. Always maintain a constant, 360-degree lookout around you, looking over your shoulder to note the position and speed of other boats. You should never jump other boats' wakes too close to their vessels or play "chicken" with other PWC.

- If two personal watercraft are passing head-on, they should always try to pass Port to Port. This topic is further discussed in Chapter 5.

- While crossing, always give way to the vessel on your right.

Liveries (Boat/PWC Rental Facilities)

Liveries rent all different types of boats and must comply with all state and federal boating laws. Many states have laws restricting who may rent boats, requiring that liveries provide instruction and identify safety equipment provided to renters. Even though the liveries may supply this information, you should still be familiar with your own state's laws and regulations. It is your responsibility to be a safe boater.

CHAPTER 2

BRING THE RIGHT EQUIPMENT

Registration, Numbering and Documentation

Boat operators need to become familiar with boating laws and regulations concerning numbering, registration and documentation. The federal government requires that all undocumented motorized vessels be numbered in the state of principle use (where you use your boat the majority of the time). Individual states may also extend these requirements to include non-motorized boats. When registering your vessel in the state of principal use, you will be issued a certificate of number. This certificate must be carried onboard the vessel whenever it is in use.

CHAPTER 2 – BRING THE RIGHT EQUIPMENT

In the event the vessel is moved to a new state of principal use, the current registration certificate will be valid for a temporary period of time allowing the owner of the vessel to transfer the registration. Although it varies between states, vessels are generally allowed to be temporarily used for a period of 60 days. In addition, states may also have titling laws and require the display of validation stickers; therefore, be sure to check with the appropriate agency in your state to ensure that you are following the proper procedures.

The certification agency must be notified within 15 days if: the vessel is transferred, destroyed, abandoned, lost, stolen or recovered; the certificate number is lost or destroyed; or the owner's address changes. If the title or registration becomes invalid for any reason, it must be surrendered in the manner prescribed to the issuing authority within 15 days.

The U.S. Coast Guard (USCG) may document some larger recreational vessels of 5 or more net tons (approximately 32' in length and above). Owners of smaller vessels may choose to document their vessels for insurance purposes. It is important to note, however, that while documentation is required for commercial vessels, a vessel can be documented as a recreational vessel. This vessel, however, must strictly be used for recreational purposes only. A documented vessel MUST carry the certificate of documentation onboard a vessel at all times. Vessels documented with the USCG are not exempt from applicable state or federal taxes, nor is its operator exempt from compliance with federal or state equipment carriage requirements.

To document your vessel with the USCG, you must demonstrate ownership of the vessel, U.S. citizenship and eligibility for the requested endorsement. Documented vessels are identified by name and the hailing port but are not exempt from state requirements. The documentation is valid for one year from the initiation date and will need to be renewed on an annual basis. Some states may require that documented vessels also be registered with the state. If you are interested in documenting your vessel, contact the USCG as well as your state agency for more information.

CHAPTER 2 – BRING THE RIGHT EQUIPMENT

Most states recognize valid registrations from other states. This concept, known as reciprocity, will allow a boater from another state to temporarily use local waters for a specified amount of time whether visiting or having recently relocated as mentioned previously. In most states, this time period is 60 days. Since requirements vary between states, be sure to check the details with the individual state you are visiting.

Display of Numbers

A registration certificate is issued and must be onboard the boat whenever the boat is operational.

1. Registration numbers must be displayed on the forward half of the vessel on both sides above the waterline. The numbers must be bold block letters at least 3 inches high in a color contrasting to the hull. Spaces or hyphens between letter and number groupings must be equal to the width of a letter other than "l" or a number other than "1".

2. The vessel registration decal (validation stickers) must be displayed within 6 inches of the registration number. With the exception of the vessel fee decal, no other letters or numbers may be displayed nearby.

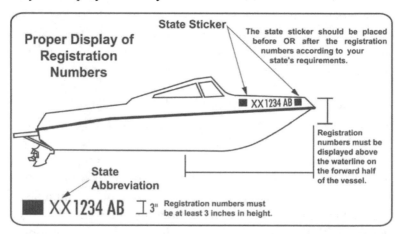

Proper Display of Registration Numbers

State Sticker
The state sticker should be placed before OR after the registration numbers according to your state's requirements.

XX 1234 AB

Registration numbers must be displayed above the waterline on the forward half of the vessel.

State Abbreviation

XX 1234 AB 3" Registration numbers must be at least 3 inches in height.

3. A documented vessel must have the name and hailing port plainly marked on the exterior part of the hull in clearly legible letters at least 4 inches in height. In addition, the vessel must

have the "Official Number" permanently affixed in block type, Arabic numerals at least 3-inches on some clearly visible interior structural part of the boat.

Hull Identification Number (HIN)

Your boat's HIN is permanently located on the outside transom of the boat hull, on the starboard side above the waterline. The boat manufacturer imprints this number. The HIN is used in the same way as a serial number on a car should your boat be lost, damaged or stolen. In most states your HIN is also required to register and title your boat.

All boats built after August 1, 1984, have to use a new HIN format, now with twelve or seventeen digits. In the twelve-digit format, the first three digits are the manufacturer's identification code. The next five digits are the hull serial number. The ninth digit indicates the month of certification or manufacturer, the tenth digit indicates the last digit of the year of manufacture and the eleventh and twelfth digits indicate the vessel's model year. Federal law stipulates that a HIN should never be altered or removed; it also requires that this number to be permanently attached to a second, unexposed location on the boat. To demonstrate proof of ownership, retain a copy this number and keep it in a safe place off the boat.

Boating Equipment

Boat Maintenance and Repair

Just like maintaining an automobile, boats require maintenance checks to keep them in top operating condition. Make it a routine practice to check your boat both on land and on water to ensure that it will operate properly. Your Owner's Manual will have a checklist of regular maintenance procedures to be followed such as oil changes, tune-ups, checking the water pump and electrical system, changing the spark plugs and cleaning the fuel filter. You should be able to perform these procedures as well as make minor repairs. Be aware that you should also replace some parts at regular intervals. If your boat is equipped with a gasoline engine, you must pay particular attention to your engine as newer blends of gasoline contain alcohol that can cause problems for plastic, rubber and metal parts in engines. Fuel hoses are most likely to lose their integrity and will need to be replaced when they show signs of cracking, leakage or become spongy, allowing explosive vapors to be released into the boat.

Become familiar with your valves, gauges, engine, fuel and electrical systems. Make sure that your battery is fully charged, and check through hull fittings for cracks and possible leakage. Check the engine for anything that requires tightening or replacing. Gauges should be operating when the engine is turned on. Valves should turn properly and attached hoses should not have kinks or cracks in them. You do not want to be on the water and have something break down as a result of infrequent maintenance. Before operating your vessel you should complete an Operations Checklist to ensure everything is in working order. Routine inspection and maintenance of your boat, its engine(s) and equipment will keep the boat in good working condition.

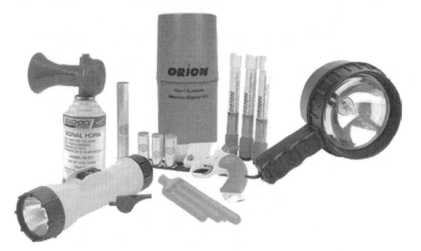

Required Safety Equipment

Federal Requirements

The U.S. Coast Guard (USCG) sets minimum standards for the required safety equipment to be carried onboard all vessels. In order for equipment to meet USCG standards, it must be labeled as

"U.S. Coast Guard-approved." When your vessel is operated on federally controlled or navigable waters, you must have all federally required boating safety equipment onboard. Navigable waters are defined as waterways that are directly connected to the ocean, so are therefore affected by tides and are capable of being navigated by vessels for the purpose of reaching the ocean. While most state boating laws require the same boating safety equipment as federal regulations, there can be some variations. Be sure to refer to your state's boating laws to ensure that you equip your boat with the appropriate safety equipment. Be aware that USCG and state marine patrol officers will frequently board boats and inspect them to enforce boating safety equipment requirements.

Backfire Flame Arrestor

The USCG requires that all gasoline engines, except outboards, be equipped with an approved and acceptable means of backfire flame control. This includes inboard engines both with and without carburetors. A backfire is when engine fuel is ignited too soon or unburned exhaust gases explode in an internal combustion engine. A backfire flame control device is attached to the engine's air intake system and disperses backfire into the atmosphere reducing the possibility for explosion or fire. In the event of an engine backfire, this device also prevents fire from leaving the intake system. The device must be suitably attached to the air intake with a flame tight connection and is required to be USCG approved or comply with SAEJ-1928 or UL 1111 standards. It is the responsibility of the boat manufacturer to install the backfire flame arrestor, but boat owners and operators should familiarize themselves with the device so they can be sure it is installed correctly and working properly.

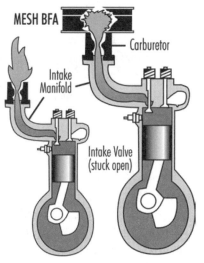

Flame Arrestor

It is also important to properly maintain the backfire flame arrestor. If you store your boat during the winter or do not use it frequently for a significant time period, you should inspect the arrestor prior to using your boat. During the boating season, clean it with grease dissolvers to keep the engine breathing properly. Make sure that all the metal elements are sealed since an arrestor with just one small gap can allow flames to pass through and start a fire in the engine. Damaged arrestors should be replaced immediately. Refer to your Owner's Manual for specific maintenance instructions.

Ventilation System

Fuel vapors are heavier than air. On many inboard and inboard/outboard powered boats, fuel vapors can accumulate in the bilge, creating an explosion hazard. Boat ventilation systems provide fresh air to areas inside the boat, removing explosive vapors from engine and fuel tank compartments. Ventilation systems can be either natural or powered. It is also the responsibility of the boat manufacturer to install the boat's ventilation system. Again, boat owners and operators should familiarize themselves with the system so they can be sure it is installed correctly and working properly.

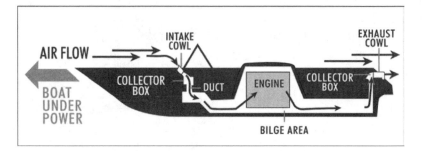

Natural ventilation systems rely on air currents to keep air circulating. According to federal law, ventilation ducts must be at least two inches in diameter. The intake ducts must be positioned midway to the bilge to keep air blowing through the bilge area, and they must be below the intake areas of the engine's carburetor. Exhaust ducts must be positioned near the bilge and connected to cowls that lead to open air.

Powered ventilation systems use blower fans and ductwork to force fuel vapors from the bilge to the atmosphere. If your boat is equipped with a powered system, it is recommended that you operate the bilge blower for at least four minutes before starting your inboard or inboard/outboard boat, to reduce the possibility of an explosion.   Each state may have different laws regarding ventilation systems.   Be sure to familiarize yourself with the requirements for appropriate ventilation systems in your state before operating your boat.

Navigation Lights

Navigation lights are used to alert others and/or indicate what another boater is doing. Recreational boats are required by law to display navigation lights between sunset and sunrise, during bad weather and in situations with reduced visibility.   It is the responsibility of the manufacturer to install navigation lights on a vessel. Boat owners and operators, however, are required to make sure they are installed correctly and are the proper configuration for the boat type and size.

Navigation lights are restricted to the colors red, green and white although the location of the lights and their size varies depending on the boat's length.   While the white light is mainly used for visibility, the purpose of the red and green navigation lights is to show if your boat is in a head-on, crossing or overtaking situation.   Knowing the 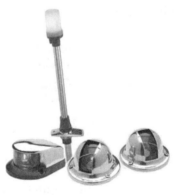 position of boats sharing the waterway with you at night will allow you to follow the "Rules of the Road" appropriately. When operating a motorboat, you are required to have a green light visible on the starboard (right) side, a red light visible on the port (left) side of the boat, and a white light located at the stern and mast or an all-around white light.

CHAPTER 2 – BRING THE RIGHT EQUIPMENT

Types of Lights

Sidelights

Sidelights are red and green lights that can be seen from a boat approaching from the side or head-on. If you see a red light it indicates you are observing the port (left) side and a green light indicates the starboard (right) side of the boat. Sidelights on boats smaller than 12 meters (40 feet) must have a 112.5-degree arc for each light and be visible for at least one mile. For boats ranging from 12 meters long to less than 50 meters (165 feet), the lights must be visible for at least two miles.

Stern light

The stern light is a white light that can be seen only behind the boat. The stern light must have a 135-degree arc and be visible for at least two miles.

Masthead light

The masthead light is a white light that shines forward and to the sides. These are required on the main mast of all sailboats and all powerboats. A masthead light must have a 225-degree arc and be visible for at least two miles on a boat under 12 meters, three miles for a boat from 12 meters (40 feet) to less than 20 meters (65 feet) in length and five miles for vessels greater than 20 meters (65 feet) to less than 50 meters (165 feet) in length.

All-round white light

All-round white lights are necessary on vessels being towed. Some powerboats may also use them instead of a combination of stern and masthead lights. This is further discussed in the next section. All-round white lights also serve as an anchor light when the sidelights are extinguished. These lights must have complete 360-degree visibility and be visible up to two miles away.

CHAPTER 2 – BRING THE RIGHT EQUIPMENT

Display of Lights

The diagrams included with the text in the following paragraphs indicate the radius and location of each type of light. The color of each light is dependent on its location on the boat as described in the previous paragraphs.

Powerboats

Motorized vessels (including sailboats operating under power) less than 50 meters (165 feet) in length must display a masthead light on the forward half of the vessel, sidelights and a stern light. Motorized vessels less than 12 meters (40 feet) in length or motorized vessels of any length being operated on the Great Lakes may display an all-around white light and sidelights instead of a masthead light, stern light and sidelights. Motorized vessels less than 7 meters (23 feet) whose speed does not exceed seven knots are only required to display an all-around white light. Motorized vessels less than 20 meters (65 feet) long, when at anchor, are required to display a white anchor light. Boats less than 7 meters (23 feet) do not have to display anchor lights unless they are anchored where other boats normally navigate or anchor.

EXAMPLES OF LIGHT DISPLAY

Motorized Vessels (including sailboats operating under power) less than 50 Meters

Motorized Vessels at anchor or less than 7 Meters

CHAPTER 2 – BRING THE RIGHT EQUIPMENT

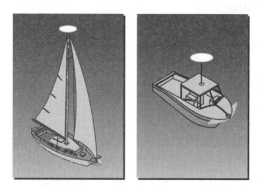

Motorized Vessels (including sailboats operating under power) less than 12 Meters

Non-motorized Vessels

Non-motorized boats less than 7 meters (23 feet) long and a vessel under oars must carry a flashlight or lighted lantern with a white light that is ready at hand to display allowing sufficient time to avoid a collision. It is also good idea to bring along extra batteries for the flashlight in case of emergency situations.

Sailboats

Sailboats under sail are required to display a green light visible on the starboard (right) side, a red light visible on the port (left) side, and white stern light. A sailboat propelled by sail alone is not required to illuminate the masthead light. Sailboats can also choose to exhibit two additional all-around lights in a vertical line at the top of the mast, the top light being red and the lower green. For sailboats less than 20 meters (65 feet) long the sidelights and stern light can be replaced with a tricolor masthead light. However, this tricolor masthead light is not to be displayed at the same time as the additional red and green all-round masthead lights.

CHAPTER 2 – BRING THE RIGHT EQUIPMENT

If it is not practical for a sailboat less than 7 meters (23 feet) long to display the configuration of lights described above, a white-lighted flashlight or lantern must be ready at hand to display in an emergency situation, allowing sufficient time to avoid a collision. Sailboats should also display an all-round white light when at anchor.

EXAMPLES OF LIGHT DISPLAY

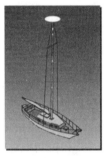

Sailboats operating under sail   **Sailboats at anchor**

Sailboats less than 7 Meters   **Sailboats less than 20 Meters**

The use of sirens or flashing, occulting or revolving lights is prohibited except where expressly allowed by law.

CHAPTER 2 – BRING THE RIGHT EQUIPMENT

Fire Extinguishers

Even though you are surrounded by water when you are boating, water will not extinguish flammable liquids. While water is a good extinguisher for garbage, mattresses, wood or rags, you should never use water on a gasoline, oil, grease or electrical fire. As an early fire warning system, all boats should have carbon monoxide detectors that will detect fumes from any gasoline-fueled appliances. For your protection, however, U.S. Coast Guard-approved fire extinguishers are required on boats where a fire hazard could be expected from a motor's fueling system.

Fire extinguishers are classified by a letter and number symbol. The letter A, B or C indicates the type of fire the extinguisher can put out. A Type A is used for trash, wood, paper; a Type B for liquids and a Type C for electrical and equipment.

The number indicates the extinguisher size in gallons or pounds. Marine type extinguishers are either B-I or B-II classification. The B-II extinguisher has a larger holding capacity than the B-I. Boats require a minimum number of hand portable fire extinguishers. Refer to the following chart to review fire extinguisher requirements.

Class	Vessel Length	No Fixed System	Approved Fixed System
1	< 26'	1 B-I	None
2	26' to <40'	2 B-I or 1 B-II	1 B-I
3	40' to <65'	3 B-I or 1 B-I and 1 B-II	2 B-I or 1 B-II

The standard is for powerboats to carry a sufficient number of fire extinguishers to meet the "No Fixed System" requirement. There is an exemption that applies to vessels that have a USCG-approved fixed fire extinguisher system ("Fixed System") in the engine compartment that allows these vessels to reduce the number of fire extinguishers carried onboard. This exemption would not be applicable to motorboats powered with outboard engines.

You should make a habit of checking your fire extinguisher prior to boating. Look to see that the seals are not broken, pressure gauges are working and no physical damage has occurred. Your extinguisher should be mounted in an accessible location for emergency situations away from areas where a fire could likely start. You should have at least one extinguisher positioned near the operator at the helm. On boats with cabins, it is also advisable to have an extinguisher readily accessible below-decks and another near the engine compartment. The extinguisher should be removed from all packaging and if possible, mounted at a location that is easy to reach. When storing your extinguishers, choose a location that you will be able to reach safely in the event of an engine fire such as the forward half of the vessel. Do not store fire extinguishers in locked compartments or under other equipment. It is important to understand how to work the fire extinguishers before an emergency occurs. You should develop an action plan that you can follow in the event of a fire.

Using a Fire Extinguisher

If a fire breaks out, take action immediately by stopping the boat and having all your passengers put on a PFD. Remember the fire triangle. Three elements, fuel, oxygen and a heat source, must be present for any fire to exist. Should you eliminate one of these three, the fire will go out. Use your fire extinguisher to put out the flames. Aim the fire extinguisher at the base of the flames, applying it to the fire in short bursts and sweeping from side to side. Prevent the fire from spreading through the boat by keeping it downwind. For example, if the fire is in the stern of the vessel direct the bow into the wind. If the engine or motor catches fire, shut off the fuel supply. Keep in mind that even if a fire seems to be dead, it could smolder for some time and then come back to life so continuously monitor the fire area. Boat fires are extremely dangerous, so it is important that you are prepared to efficiently handle this type of an emergency.

Visual Distress Signals

Visual Distress Signals (VDSs) are used to signal for help in the case of an emergency. There are two main types of VDSs, day and night signals. They are also either pyrotechnic (using flame) or non-pyrotechnic. All boaters should be able to signal for help. Boaters must be equipped with U.S. Coast Guard (USCG) approved visual distress signals that are in proper working order, and not beyond their expiration date. The following vessels are not required to carry day signals, but must carry night signals when operating from sunset to sunrise:

1. Recreational boats less than 16 feet in length.

2. Boats participating in organized events such as races, regattas, or marine parades.

3. Open sailboats less than 26 feet in length not equipped with propulsion machinery.

4. Manually propelled boats.

The USCG has approved Pyrotechnic and Non-Pyrotechnic Visual Distress Signals and associated devices. They include a variety of types as indicated in the following pictures.

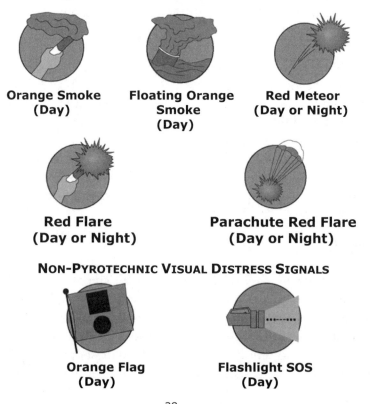

PYROTECHNIC VISUAL DISTRESS SIGNALS

Orange Smoke (Day)　　**Floating Orange Smoke (Day)**　　**Red Meteor (Day or Night)**

Red Flare (Day or Night)　　**Parachute Red Flare (Day or Night)**

NON-PYROTECHNIC VISUAL DISTRESS SIGNALS

Orange Flag (Day)　　**Flashlight SOS (Day)**

All vessels larger than 16 feet must carry approved VDSs for both day and night time use. Non-Pyrotechnic Visual Distress Signals must be in serviceable condition, readily accessible and certified by the manufacturer as complying with USCG requirements. VDSs should be removed from all packaging and stored in a location that is easy to reach in the event of an emergency. Do not store VDSs in a locked compartment or under other equipment.

Note that the rules above refer to boats being operated in U.S. Coastal waters, including the Great Lakes System, oceans and any bay or sound that empties into the ocean and adjoining rivers two miles wide or more at the mouth up to the first point of the river that narrows to less than two miles wide. State laws may differ from the U.S. Coast Guard requirements. It's important to check with your state boating agency or local law enforcement officials to learn the specific rules for VDS usage in your local waters.

Sound Producing Devices

Your boat must be equipped with a sound-producing device (such as a horn, or whistle) that is capable of producing a 4 to 6 second blast audible for at least 1/2 mile. Large vessels, 12 meters (39 feet) or greater, must carry a bell and a whistle or horn. The bell must be at least 7.87 inches (200 mm) in diameter. Using these signaling devices will be further discussed in the Rules of the Road Section of Chapter 5.

Personal Flotation Devices (PFDs)

Life jackets, also known as PFDs, are a piece of required safety equipment. When PFDs are worn, they can provide the buoyancy you need to stay afloat and, when used correctly, can save lives in the event of a man overboard or capsized vessel emergency. PFDs are available in many different types and styles and are sized based on body weight and chest size. It is a federal requirement that all boats, regardless of size, must carry at least one wearable PFD of the appropriate size (Type I, II, III or Type V) for every person onboard. Boats longer than 16 feet must also carry at least one throwable (Type IV) flotation device. Since there are many different types and styles of flotation devices, make sure that the PFDs carried on your vessel are the appropriate size and type for your passengers and the boating activity.

Because of leading innovations in flotation technology, PFD manufacturers are continuously updating their materials and design. PFDs today are more comfortable to wear, have improved breathability and even look better than traditional models. A few examples of these PFDs are included in Chapter 1 with the Water Activities section. Visit your local watersports or boating store to check out additional models that best suit your needs.

Choosing the Right PFD

In order for a PFD to be used properly, it must be the correct size for the wearer, be appropriate for the boating activity and be in good condition. PFDs should also be readily accessible for use. This includes removing them from all packaging and keeping them near you so that you can put it on quickly in the event of an emergency. Do not keep your PFDs in a locked compartment or under other stored equipment. If you are boating with both children and adults, be sure to have PFDs available on your vessel that are the appropriate size for all of the passengers. Since all PFDs are not approved for every boating activity, even if they are USCG approved, always read the label of the PFD to determine any restrictions for the PFDs use. For example, Type III and V inflatables are approved for boaters at least 16 years of age but must be worn in order to be considered USCG-approved. Inflatables are not approved for operating a PWC, water-skiing or whitewater rafting. This is because these activities often result in a forcefully hitting the water, which could cause an inflatable PFD to unintentionally inflate and potentially cause injury to the wearer. While many people prefer wearing inflatable PFDs since they are less bulky than PFDs with buoyant material, they must be used appropriately in order to be effective.

CHAPTER 2 – BRING THE RIGHT EQUIPMENT

Maintaining Your PFD

It is also important that you follow the directions on the PFD's label regarding proper maintenance. You should routinely inspect your PFDs for rips or tears in the fabric and sun bleach that may result in the PFD losing buoyancy. Make sure that all the straps, buckles and zippers are working properly. Following use, allow your PFD to drip-dry thoroughly. Never lay it to dry on a radiator, heater or direct heat source. Also, stow it in a well-ventilated place to prevent mildew. PFDs that are not in good condition or have labels that are unreadable should be replaced. In addition to a basic inspection, Type III and Type V inflatable PFDs should always be checked for air holes before use and be maintained per the manufacturer's recommendations. To check for air holes, blow up the PFD using the manual inflation valve and then submerge it in water. Make sure that the Carbon Dioxide cartridge is full and has not been inflated by mistake. You want to make sure the PFD is operational in case it is needed.

Wearing Your PFD

Federal Law requires that PFDs be worn while water skiing or being towed behind a boat or another aquaplaning device. Federal Law also requires that all children under the age of 13 wear a USCG-approved PFD while on a recreational vessel that is underway unless they are in an enclosed cabin or below deck. This law as well as all other federal boating regulations are applicable when your vessel is being operated on waters under federal jurisdiction, including coastal waters greater than 3 miles away from the Atlantic and Pacific coasts and gulf waters greater than 9 miles away from the Gulf of Mexico coasts as well as navigable lakes and rivers such as the Great Lakes and Mississippi Rivers System. Waters within 3 miles of the Atlantic and Pacific coasts and 9 miles of the Gulf of Mexico coasts as well as inland lakes are under state jurisdiction. Since states vary in their boating regulations including mandatory PFD usage, be sure to check with your state agency to ensure that you are following all the applicable laws.

CHAPTER 2 – BRING THE RIGHT EQUIPMENT

Although federal and state laws require some persons to wear their PFDs, it is highly advisable that all boaters wear their PFDs at all times. Wearing your PFD while boating or involved in a water activity could save your life. Emergency situations often

arise unexpectedly and if you are wearing your PFD when the situation occurs, you will be better prepared to deal with the circumstances. To stay safe, boat operators should be alert to changes in boating conditions and inform their passengers to put on their PFDs in dangerous situations. Remember that because of their buoyancy, PFDs are difficult to put on in the water. It is recommended that boaters wear their PFDs during any of the following conditions:

- Severe weather

  Examples of severe weather include high winds, rain, hail or thunderstorms.

- Dangerous water conditions

  Examples of dangerous water conditions include increased wave height or strong currents.

- While boating at a distance from shore

  You should wear your PFD when you are boating at a distance from shore where you could not easily swim to shore in the event of an emergency. When determining if you are within swimming distance of shore, do not forget to take into consideration that the shore often appears closer than it actually is and that there may be offshore currents that are not easily distinguishable. You should also take into consideration your physical fitness level when determining if you should swim to shore.

- Times of high boat traffic

  Examples of high boat traffic include operating a boat with other vessels in a narrow inlet, small lake or any other constrained water body, during a marine event or any other situation where you must anchor or moor offshore close to other vessels or during the time of day such as early morning or late afternoon where there is a likelihood of a number of other vessels operating in the same area as you.

- While operating at night

  If you are operating at a time when your navigation lights are illuminated, you should wear your PFD. Since it is difficult to distinguish a man overboard from the water during nighttime, a PFD will assist rescuers in locating you and will keep you afloat until help arrives.

- While boating alone

  If you are boating alone, you will be responsible for your own safety and taking the appropriate action in the event of an emergency. Since there is no one else onboard your vessel that can help you, you should wear your PFD to increase your chance of survival if you fall overboard or your vessel capsizes.

- While experiencing local hazards

  Examples of local hazards include rocky shoals or shallow areas that you must avoid to prevent running aground, currents due to tidal changes, narrow inlets, and areas that are difficult to navigate such as tight corners or channel forks.

CHAPTER 2 – BRING THE RIGHT EQUIPMENT

PFD Checklist

To enforce equipment requirements, the USCG and Marine Patrols frequently board boats for routine inspections. During inspections your boat will be checked for the following concerning PFDs:

1. The proper number, type, and size of PFDs.

   - Is it USCG approved?

   - Is it designed for your chest size and weight?

   - Is the PFD type suitable for the type of boating you are doing?

2. The condition of the PFD. A PFD is only good if kept in proper condition while stored on your boat. Again, be sure to replace if there is excessive wear or damage.

   - Do not place heavy objects on your PFD or use it as a fender. PFDs lose buoyancy when they are crushed.

   - Only wear your PFD. Do not use it to cushion yourself or other boats.

3. Convenient storage and access to your flotation device.

   - Store inflatable PFDs per the manufacturer's recommendations.

   - Remove your PFD from the plastic after purchasing.

   - If you are not wearing your PFD, keep it in an easily accessible location so in the event of an emergency you can grab it quickly.

4. A throwable device onboard.

CHAPTER 2 – BRING THE RIGHT EQUIPMENT

- Practice your knots discussed in Chapter 4 on a life ring, horseshoe buoy or buoyant cushion, and then practice throwing the device.

Types of PFDs

Type I (Offshore Life Jacket)

- Vest or yoke type life jackets are required to be orange in color.

- They come in two sizes: adult and child.

- The adult size has a minimum of 22 lbs. of flotation.

- The child size provides a minimum of 11 lbs. of flotation.

- *Advantages:* These devices are effective in all waters, especially where rescue may be delayed, as they are designed to turn most unconscious wearers in the water to a face-up position.

- *Disadvantages:* Can be bulky and uncomfortable to wear for long periods of time.

Type II (Near-Shore Buoyant Vest)

- Intended for calm, inland water and usually looks like a bib with a collar behind the neck.

- Type II has a minimum of: 15.5 lbs. of flotation for adults, 11 lbs. for a medium size child, and 7 lbs. for an infant or x-small size child.

- *Advantages:* This type of life jacket will turn some unconscious wearers to a face-up position. They are less bulky than a Type I PFD and more comfortable to wear.

- *Disadvantages:* Will not turn as many wearers into a face-up position as a Type I PFD. Are not intended for use in rough waters.

Type III (Flotation Aid)

- These devices are also intended for calm inland water.

- They are designed so wearers can place themselves in a face-up position.

- The Type III has the same minimum flotation standards as Type II.

- Some are designed as inflatables.

- *Advantages:* This type of PFD is generally the most comfortable to wear. Many are designed to protect the wearer in the event of a water impact and have associated impact ratings.

- *Disadvantages:* This type of PFD will not turn most unconscious wearers in a face-up position.

Type IV (Throwable Devices)

- These devices are used in calm, inland water where help is always available.

- This life preserver is designed to be thrown to a person in the water.

- These life preservers are not designed to be worn.

- Some examples are life rings, horseshoe buoys and buoyant cushions.

- *Advantages:* This type of PFD can be easily thrown to a person in the water. Is a good secondary safety device in addition to wearable PFDs.

- *Disadvantages:* This type of PFD cannot be used to rescue unconscious persons. It is also not intended to rescue non-swimmers or children or for long periods of use.

Type V (Special Use Device)

- May be carried instead of another PFD, if used in accordance with the manufacturer's label.

- Some provide significant hypothermia protection.

- Some are designed as inflatables.

- *Advantages:* This type of PFD is the least bulky of all the types. They are designed to be worn continually.

- *Disadvantages:* Type V inflatables require active use and care of the inflation cartridge. They also have to be worn in order to meet USCG requirements.

Recommended Safety Equipment

Cooling Systems

To prevent engines from overheating, boats are equipped with cooling systems. The cooling system draws in water from under the boat, circulates it to cool the engine and discharges the water through the engine's exhaust system. Some inboard/outboards and inboard engines have a closed cooling system that circulates water through a heat transfer process similar to a car's radiator.

CHAPTER 2 – BRING THE RIGHT EQUIPMENT

First Aid Kit

A prepared boater should include a First Aid Kit as part of the necessary boating equipment. Boating injuries can occur and having a First Aid Kit onboard will assist you in treating that injury.

Communication Equipment

It is a good idea to carry a means of communication with you while boating.

Choices include:

- Cell phone (limited range)

- VHF marine radio (excellent choice, good range)

- CB radio (good range)

- EPIRB (directs rescuers to you in case of emergency)

While cell phones provide a form of backup communications, it is important not to rely on them entirely. If you opt to carry a cell phone, have phone numbers listed for use in an emergency situation. A VHF marine radio is highly recommended for boaters because many towing companies and boating law enforcement agencies (including the U.S. Coast Guard) monitor VHF channel 16.

Carrying a radio onboard vessels under 65 feet or 20 meters in length is not a requirement. However, if one is carried the rules of the Federal Communications Commission (FCC) must be followed. In an emergency situation, contact the U.S. Coast Guard through your VHF marine radio using distress channel 16. Use a MAYDAY signal for life threatening situations only.

You will also give:

- Vessel name and/or description

- Position and/or location

- Nature of emergency

- Number of people onboard

If you are hailing a nearby vessel, use channel 16 to get their attention and then agree to change to another frequency to continue the conversation. Do not attempt to hail a vessel for longer than 30 seconds.

Anchors

All boats, regardless of size, are advised to carry an anchor. Anchoring will keep you from drifting should your engine fail or you run aground in bad weather. They also allow you to "park" so that you can enjoy your surroundings. If a mooring buoy is available in the area you are boating, use it before an anchor. The use of mooring buoys will prevent your anchor from damaging the environment.

Types of Anchors

- Plow Anchors work well in weeds, sand, mud & gravel.

- Grapnel Anchors, due to their design, are used primarily for snagging on rocky bottoms or trees.

- A Mushroom anchor is a good anchor for permanent moorings in calm waters. It tends to sink deeply into the bottom when left for long periods.

- Lightweight Anchors have stronger holding power because they bury themselves in soft sand, mud and gravel. They do not work well in grassy, clay or rocky bottoms.

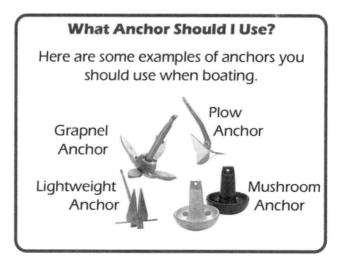

What Anchor Should I Use?

Here are some examples of anchors you should use when boating.

Grapnel Anchor

Plow Anchor

Lightweight Anchor

Mushroom Anchor

Nautical Charts

Nautical Charts are maps for the boater. These charts show the nature and shape of the coast, water depth, bottom contours, prominent landmarks, ports and facilities. Charts also are aids to navigation, marine hazards and other pertinent information.

Nautical charts assist the boater in identifying potentially hazardous conditions, such as shallow waters. Through the use of nautical charts, one of the most common types of boat accidents, boat groundings, can easily be prevented. Due to the frequency of groundings and the need to protect our marine resources, many states and National Parks are fining boat operators responsible for grounding their boat in a protected area. Keep in mind when operating your boat on autopilot that autopilot does not alter its course to account for shallow waters.

Changes in topography and in the waterways necessitate that nautical charts be periodically updated to offer the most current information. Only up-to-date charts should be used for navigation. Nautical charts can be purchased either online or at your local marine retail store. Chart updating information can be obtained from "Local Notice to Mariners" published by the U.S. Coast

Guard. Before boating, be sure to study a nautical chart of the area where you will be operating your vessel to ensure the safety of both your boat and the environment.

Global Positioning System

Boaters can use a Global Positioning System (GPS) to determine their location. A GPS is an electronic piece of equipment that uses satellites to determine longitude and latitude. Accuracy depends on the unit model but good GPS units can be accurate to a few hundred feet. Carrying a GPS is highly beneficial for the boater as it greatly assists in navigation and in emergency situations. During an emergency, a GPS allows boaters to quickly relay accurate location information to rescuers or emergency responders. However, since GPS are battery powered, boaters should also familiarize themselves with more traditional means of navigation in order to ensure they will not be lost if their GPS unit dies.

Compass

A compass is a more traditional method of navigation that has been used by boaters for centuries. This instrument indicates directionality based on the earth's magnetic fields. Since the earth's magnetism varies based on location, a compass indicates magnetic north. When charting or plotting a course using a compass, the boater must calculate true north by using corrections found on nautical charts or in navigational books. Learning to steer using a compass can be a valuable tool in situations where a GPS is not working, visibility is reduced or land is out of sight. To ensure accurate compass readings, do not use them near iron, magnets or electrical wiring and equipment, as these can influence the compass' magnetism.

CHAPTER 3

LEAVING THE DOCK

Getting Ready to Go

Pre-Departure Checklist

Before leaving the dock, it is important to do a preliminary check of your boat's systems and orient your passengers to the location of the emergency equipment and basic functions of the boat. Your pre-departure checklist should at least include the following tasks:

1. Check to make sure you have all of the equipment required by both federal and state regulations.

2. Check your engine's oil and fluid levels. Make sure you have a full fuel tank.

3. Make sure battery connections are tight and the battery is fully charged.

4. Make sure there is a PFD onboard for every passenger and the PFDs are the right size for their users.

5. Make sure emergency, communication, and visual distress equipment are current (if applicable) and operational.

6. Inform your passengers of the locations of PFDs, Fire Extinguishers, Flares and First Aid Kit and how to operate the radio in an emergency

7. Show your passengers how to use the head (marine toilet) properly, handle lines, operate the boat in an emergency or rough weather conditions, anchor and what to do in a man-overboard situation.

8. An example of a Pre-Departure Checklist is included in the back of this manual.

Float Plan

Before leaving the dock on your boat, you should be sure to inform a local marina, relative or friend of your plans. It is always a good idea to file a float plan and have someone on shore that knows your plans and will take action if you fail to return on time. For short day trips, you can file a "casual" float plan by contacting a friend or family member and telling them where you will be boating and when you plan to return. Be sure to leave a phone number for local authorities as well as a date and time to contact the authorities if you have not yet returned from your trip. Always notify this person if your plans change and when you return home. For longer trips, leave a detailed information list describing the size and type of your vessel, its registration number, tow vehicle's license plate number (if applicable), trip itinerary, and expected time of return. Also include a list of all your passengers and an emergency contact for each of them. Your onshore contact will be able to notify the U.S. Coast Guard (USCG) or other rescue organizations should you not return as scheduled. Inform your contact should you be delayed in your return. The contact should be aware that if you do not return as scheduled and it is approaching dusk, the call to alert appropriate authorities should be made sooner rather than later due to limited daylight. An example of a float plan is included in the back of this manual.

Fueling Procedures

Fueling is an important part of the boating process and should be undertaken with great care. Following improper fueling procedures could result in property damage, serious injury or even death. Before you begin fueling, stop all engines, motors, fans or other motorized devices that might produce sparks. If you operate a cabin motorboat, close all ports, windows, doors and hatches to keep volatile fumes from entering the cabin of your boat. During fueling, keep the nozzle of the fuel hose in contact with the fill opening to guard against possible static spark. Do not smoke, strike matches or throw switches when fueling. Be careful that no fuel spills into the boat hull or bilge. After fueling is complete, close the fill opening tightly, wipe up any fuel spills and open the ports, windows, doors and hatches, allowing the boat to ventilate for at least five minutes. If your vessel is equipped with a powered ventilation system or blower, run the blower for at least four minutes. Before starting your engine, perform a sniff test to make sure there is no gas odor in the engine room or any other compartment on your boat. Remember that if your vessel is equipped with a bilge, this is where gasoline fumes are most likely to accumulate. You should make sure to keep your bilge clean and free of trash to reduce the risk of a fire. If you are filling a portable fuel tank, do not fill the tank while it is on the boat. Instead, take the tanks ashore to be filled. When filling the tank, do not set it on the side of your boat or towing vehicle. Make sure it is firmly balanced on the ground to avoid accidental fuel spills. If possible, you should fuel your boat away from the water. This is because fuel can be harmful to the environment if it enters the waterway. Protecting your marine environment while fueling is further discussed in Chapter 6.

Trailering Your Boat

If your boat is not kept at a dock, you will probably need to become familiar with and understand how to load, tow, launch and retrieve your boat. Your boat's length, weight and hull style are all factors when selecting a boat trailer. Most boat dealers will assist you in choosing a boat trailer.

A boat trailer is designed to support the boat securely while the boat is being transported. Make sure your vehicle is capable of towing the trailer. Trailers have both a carrying capacity (how much weight it can carry) and gross vehicle weight rating (the carrying capacity plus the weight of the trailer). The trailer should be rated a weight that is sufficient to carry the boat, engine and any gear such as boating safety equipment that will be carried onboard while it is being towed. The standard rule of thumb is that a boat should weigh less than 90% of a trailer's carrying capacity. If the boat weighs 90% of the trailer's carrying capacity, a larger trailer should be used. The Owner's Manual of the tow vehicle will give its tow rating maximum that should be matched with the trailer's gross vehicle weight rating.

The trailer is attached to the towing vehicle by using a hitch. Hitches come in different shapes and sizes, but the most common is a ball hitch that is attached to your automobile. The tongue of the trailer has a coupler that fits over the ball hitch. It is important to remember that the size of the coupler must match the size of the ball hitch. A ball hitch has a tongue weight stamped onto the ball indicating the amount of weight a loaded trailer places on the hitch of the tow vehicle. If the tongue of the trailer is too heavy, the tow vehicle's steering will be negatively impacted. If there is too little weight on the hitch, the trailer will begin to sway. The tongue weight should be 7 to 10 percent of the combined weight of the trailer and boat.

CHAPTER 3 – LEAVING THE DOCK

Two safety chains should be part of your trailer equipment, and these chains must be strong enough to maintain control of the trailer if the hitch or coupling breaks. These chains are hooked between the frame of your automobile and the trailer in the form of an "X", and should be long enough to allow the trailer to  turn but not so long that they drag on the ground when the vehicle is in motion. The chain's strength needs to be 1.5 times the maximum gross trailer weight. Licensing and lighting requirements may vary in individual states. Contact your state's Department of Motor Vehicles for detailed boat trailer regulations.

Driving With A Trailer

When driving a vehicle towing a trailer, you should operate cautiously, considering the effect that the trailer may have on the safe operation of your towing vehicle. Observing the following practices when trailering will help you to safely arrive at the boat ramp for a fun day on the water:

- You should drive at a slower speed in order to keep the trailer under control. Driving at high speeds while towing could cause the trailer to sway and could result in you losing control of your towing vehicle. Consequently, the trailer could overturn or you could be involved in an accident with another vehicle in another lane of traffic.

- When turning, you should make wider turns to avoid running over curbs and causing danger to pedestrian traffic.

- Be aware that the combined weight of your towing vehicle and trailer will require you to allow greater distance and more time to stop.

- When passing other vehicles, be aware of the length added by your trailer to your towing vehicle. Be careful not to cut off other drivers.

- If you are towing a trailer for a long period, you should periodically stop and check the trailer for any damage or wear and tear to rigging, tires and bearings.

Launching

Before launching your boat, you should disconnect your trailer lights since they will burst when they are heated and then submerged in water. You should also make sure that you have put the plugs securely in your bilge. If the plugs are not firmly in place, your boat will quickly fill with water. When backing up, the trailer wheels and the wheels of the tow vehicle do not follow the same path. It is important to remember that the trailer will turn in the opposite direction of the tow vehicle. Maneuvering your trailer and tow vehicle efficiently takes practice. Practice backing up the trailer before you take it to the boat launch ramp. When launching your vessel, be sure that someone onshore holds a line attached to the vessel to prevent it from drifting away from the launch ramp. Following these simple steps will ensure that you have a great start to your day on the water.

Loading

When loading your boat, you should always keep safety in mind. Here are a number of things you should remember when loading your boat:

- Hand the boat supplies to someone who is already in the boat.

- Distribute the weight or load evenly.

- Make sure all passengers remain seated.

- Fasten equipment and gear to prevent shifting while underway.

- Do not exceed the U.S. Coast Guard Maximum Capacities listed on the boat's capacity plate.

Capacity Plate

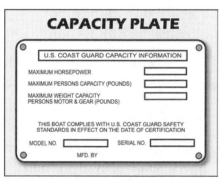

It is required for all monohull boats under 20 feet built on or after November 1, 1972 to have a capacity plate approved by the U.S. Coast Guard (USCG). In addition, some manufacturers voluntarily install capacity plates on boats larger than 20 feet. This plate must be visible from the operator's station. The capacity plate lists a safe motor size, the maximum number of persons to be carried onboard and the total weight the boat can carry including persons, motor and gear. When operating your boat be sure to adhere to the restrictions listed on the capacity plate. Not only is it dangerous to overpower or overload a small boat since they can swamp or capsize more easily, but it is also illegal. In addition, overloaded boats will be more difficult to control. In many states, there are fines and penalties for exceeding capacity recommendations, including carrying more than the maximum number of people.

For vessels that are not equipped with a capacity plate, the following formula can be used to calculate the number of persons (averaging 150 lbs each) the vessel can carry safely in good weather: **Number of people = vessel length (feet) X vessel width (feet) ÷ 15**

For example, if you are operating a 16 foot boat with a 6 foot beam (width) the maximum number of people the boat can hold would be calculated as follows:

Number of people = (16 ft X 6)/15 = 6.4

Therefore, the maximum number of people that can be safely carried on this boat in good weather would be six.

Retrieving

When retrieving the boat from the water, remember to again disconnect the trailer lights. Back the trailer into water so that 2/3 of the rollers are submerged and set the emergency brake. Navigate the boat onto the trailer so the winch cable can be attached properly. Pull the boat onto the trailer by cranking the winch, and then attach the winch's safety chain to the trailer, as a precaution should the winch malfunction. Before leaving the boat ramp, make sure your boat is securely attached to your trailer, and the trailer to the tow vehicle. Once your boat is secured on the trailer, the first thing you should do is pull the trailer well away from the boat ramp as a courtesy to other boaters, allowing them access to the water body. After you have moved your trailer away from the boat ramp, be sure to reconnect the trailer lights. You should also clean your boat before leaving the ramp to prevent the spread of aquatic nuisance species.

U.S. Aids to Navigation (ATON)

Most people are so conditioned by highway signs and signals that they read them almost automatically. They hardly think about a stoplight, a yield sign or an exit sign; and they automatically respond to the given signal. Such actions are called conditioned responses. Driving or riding in a car is so much a part of our way of life that even people who do not know how to drive a car respond to traffic signals the same way that experienced drivers do.

Photograph Provided by Paul Engle

Buoys and markers are the highway signs and signals that guide boat operators safely. The U.S. Aids to Navigation System uses lateral navigation markers and non-lateral markers to tell you where you should be in relation to the channel so that you can navigate safely and confidently.

CHAPTER 3 – LEAVING THE DOCK

This system was developed to govern boat traffic flow and prevent collisions. Be sure to familiarize yourself with the area where you will be boating and know your boat's ability to safely navigate the waters.

Non-Lateral Markers (Information and Regulatory Markers)

Uniform Waterway Markers, also known as Non-Lateral Markers, are used to notify boaters of some restriction. The most common non-lateral markers are white with orange horizontal bands on the top and bottom and black markings. They can be either buoys or posted signs.

These are examples of some of the markers you will see in the waterways:

Diamond Shape

This sign warns of danger and marks objects that may cause damage to your boat. When seeing this sign you must proceed with caution.

Diamond Shape with Cross

This sign advises the boater that the entrance into this area with a vessel of any type is prohibited. An example of this is a sign designating a swimming area.

Square or Rectangle Shape

This sign displays non-regulatory information such as directions, fuel and dockage, and marinas.

Circle Shape

This sign indicates a controlled area and indicates the action required for this area. Examples include:

Slow Speed - Minimum Wake

Any vessel operating in a speed zone posted as "Slow Speed - Minimum Wake" must operate fully off plane and completely settled in water. The vessel's wake must not be excessive nor create a hazard to other vessels.

Idle Speed – No-Wake

Any vessel operating in a speed zone posted as "Idle Speed – No-Wake" must operate at the minimum speed possible, while still being able to steer the boat.

Resume Normal Safe Operation

This indicates speed restrictions have ended and the vessel may resume a normal safe operating speed for conditions.

Lateral Markers

Lateral markers are the navigation signals in the water to mark safe water and to assist mariners in determining their position in relation to land and hidden dangers. They come in various sizes, shapes and colors. They will often be marked with a number, letter or a combination of numbers and letters. These numbers should match your nautical charts. Lateral markers can also be either lighted or unlighted. Lighted buoys flash in a regular pattern. These patterns are also indicated on nautical charts to assist boaters in identifying the buoys at a distance.

CHAPTER 3 – LEAVING THE DOCK

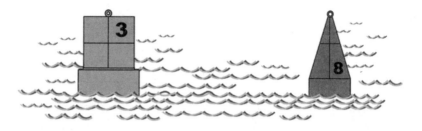

Can Buoy

These buoys are cylindrical in shape with a flat top and are always marked with green markings and odd numbers. They denote the left side of the channel when you are returning from the open sea or heading upstream.

Nun Buoy

These buoys are the same size as a can buoy except they taper upward from the waterline to create a cone shape. They are always marked with red markings and even numbers and denote the right side of the channel when you are returning from the open sea or heading upstream.

Buoy Colors and Numbers

Port Side Aids

These buoys or markers are stationed on the left side of channel denoting the boater is returning from the open sea or heading upstream. They are green in color and marked with an odd number. If lighted, they are indicated by a green light. The numbers usually increase consecutively from the open sea.

Starboard Side Aids

These buoys or markers are stationed on the right side of the channel denoting the boater is returning from the open sea or heading upstream. They are red in color and marked with an even number. If lighted, they are indicated by a red light. The numbers usually increase consecutively from the open sea.

Safe Water Markers

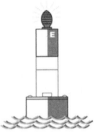

Also known as Mid-Channel Markers, Safe Water Markers have vertical red and white stripes. They can be in the form of a lighted or unlighted buoy, a daymarker or a round buoy. If lighted, the light will be white. These buoys are not numbered but may be lettered. When one of these buoys is sighted, it indicates the middle of the channel and unobstructed water on all sides. They may be passed on either side.

Preferred Channel Markers

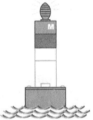

In some instances, a channel may be indicated with a lateral marker that has both red and green horizontal bands on the top. These are known as preferred channel markers. They are not numbered, but may be lettered. They also may be lighted, unlighted or in the form of a daymarker. Even though this marker appears to be confusing, it merely indicates that while boaters can operate on either side of the buoy in this area, there is a preferred channel. The color band on the top of the buoy indicates the direction of the preferred channel. Applying this knowledge, a buoy with a red horizontal band on the top followed by a green horizontal band should be viewed as a starboard side aid. It should be kept to the starboard (right) side of the vessel when returning from open water. Conversely, buoys with a green horizontal band on the top followed by a red horizontal band should be treated as port side aids and be kept on the port (left) side of the boat when returning from open ocean.

Daybeacons

Daybeacons are on fixed structures either in shallow water or on the shore. They are usually positioned on the left and right side of the channels. A green square daybeacon is similar to a can buoy, and a red triangle daybeacon is similar to a nun buoy.

CHAPTER 3 – LEAVING THE DOCK

Intracoastal Waterway Markers

The Intracoastal Waterway (ICW) is a toll free waterway that is 3,000 miles long. It stretches along the Atlantic Coast from Boston, Massachusetts to Key West, Florida and along the Gulf of Mexico coast from Apalachee Bay, Florida to Brownsville, Texas. When traveling in the ICW, buoys and markers are identified with a yellow symbol. Markers with a yellow triangle should be kept on your starboard (right) side when you are heading in a southerly direction. The opposite is true for a marker displaying a yellow square. This marker should be kept on your port (left) side when passing.

Western Rivers System Markers

The Western Rivers System of markers is present on the Mississippi River and its tributaries. The markers within this system are similar to U.S. Aids to Navigation System lateral markers except these markers are not numbered. This system of markers identifies distance from the mouth of the river, by placing a sign below the daybeacon indicating the number of miles traveled. One exception is found on the Ohio River where the number of miles identifies the distance traveled from the headwaters instead of the mouth of the river.

An easy way to remember how to pass the buoys on the proper side is "Red, Right, Returning" when you are returning from sea. This means the red buoys should always be on your right (starboard) side when returning to port or when you are going up the river. If you are leaving port or going down a river, the red buoys should be on your left (port) side. When operating in the Intracoastal Waterway, keep the red buoys on your right (starboard) side when you are traveling south.

Navigation Tips

Night Navigation

At night, you should use navigation lights to know where and how a boat is positioned. Follow the same Rules of the Road as you would during the day. Of course, you should always operate at a slower speed and be on the look out for other vessels during times of restricted visibility, such as navigating in fog, storms or around tight corners. Use the sound signals prescribed by the Navigation Rules. These rules are described in Chapter 5 of this manual.

Safe Operation

A boat operator is ultimately responsible for the safety of all the passengers onboard, the boat and any damage the boat's wake might cause to another vessel and property ashore. To ensure a safe enjoyable boating experience for yourself, your passengers and other boaters, you should observe the tips described in the following sections.

Practice good seamanship

The person driving the boat is responsible for the safety of everyone onboard. He/She must monitor the boat traffic around his boats and conduct his boat accordingly. Avoid taking unnecessary risks that could endanger life, limb or property. If you allow another person to operate your vessel, complete an operations checklist with him, giving him an overview of the vessel's basic functions, how to operate it safely and where the boating safety equipment is located, ensuring that he knows the basics of safe boating.

Keep a sharp look out

Keeping a look out will prevent most collisions. It is important to look out for other boats, others involved in water activities and navigational hazards including objects in the water.

CHAPTER 3 – LEAVING THE DOCK

Maintain a safe speed

You must maintain a safe speed and a sufficient distance from other boats, shorelines or any other object, which allows you to take the necessary action to avoid a collision and stop within an appropriate distance. If waves get large, traffic increases, or bad weather moves in, reducing your speed and navigating with caution will help keep everyone safe. When determining a speed that is safe for the prevailing conditions, you should consider the following conditions:

- Amount of boat traffic including those vessels such as barges or fishing vessels that may be restricted in their ability to maneuver

- Visibility

- If at night, any background light that may cause difficulty in identifying shapes or seeing other vessels

- The maneuverability of the vessel being operated considering the distance needed to stop safely or turn

- Sea state, wind and current

- Distance from potential navigational hazards

- The depth of water the vessel can safely be operated in without running aground or causing damage to the local aquatic or marine environment.

Be a courteous boater

Be aware of your surroundings and other boaters near you. Be careful to control your wake so as not to swamp or capsize smaller boats such as kayaks or canoes. Give fishermen a wide berth so that you will not cut their fishing lines or upset their boats with your wake. If you are fishing or hunting, do not crowd other boaters enjoying the same activity. When boating in a residential area, control your boat noise so as not to be offensive to the local community. Do not moor or anchor your boat close to a stranger's property unless given permission. When launching your boat on a boat ramp, do initial launch preparations away from the ramp so as not to impede launching for others. If another boater signals for help or assistance, be sure to see if there is anything that you can do. Being respectful to others while boating allows everyone to have fun on the water.

Theft Prevention

To protect yourself in the event of boat theft you should maintain the appropriate documentation for your vessel. Keep copies of your registration, certificate of number and your original title in a safe place off your vessel. Make a note of your HIN number since this is used to track your vessel. It is also a good idea to take photos of your boat so that you can provide them to the appropriate authorities and/or insurance companies. To reduce the risk of your vessel being stolen:

- Store your boat and trailer in locked storage area.

- Secure your boat to a mooring with steel cable and lock.

- Put identification marks on equipment and photograph the interior and exterior of your boat.

Homeland Security

Boaters should be aware of and comply with new Homeland Security measures set forth by federal, state, and local governments. These should include, but are not limited to, keeping a safe prescribed distance from military and commercial ships and avoiding commercial port operations areas, observing all security zones and following guidelines for appropriate conduct, such as not stopping or anchoring beneath bridges or in a channel.

Due to the vast amount of shoreline in our country, the U.S. Coast Guard has also recognized that boaters or other people near the water are more likely to observe a potential security threat than a U.S. Coast Guard officer. Because of this fact, the U.S. Coast

CHAPTER 3 – LEAVING THE DOCK

Guard has now implemented a national program that asks those on or near the water to be aware of suspicious activity that might indicate threats to our country's homeland security. Areas of particular concern are ports, docks, marinas, riversides, beaches, or shore communities. When near the waterfront or boating near terminals, tankers, or cruise ships boaters should watch for:

- People engaged in surveillance, taking notes or pictures and asking questions

- People who do not look like they belong near critical maritime facilities

- Strange items either being placed in or recovered from the water

- Unattended vehicles or boats in strange places

- Lights flashing between vessels

- Unusual diving activity

- Unusual people or numbers of people aboard a boat

- Strange night operations

- Boats in an unusual passage or anchorage

- Transfers of people or objects at unusual places

- Persons attempting to rent a boat with cash for short term undefined uses

- Small planes flying over critical areas or passages

If you observe any of these suspicious activities, you should contact the National Response Center at (800) 424-8802. You can also use your VHF Radio to hail the U.S. Coast Guard on Channel 16. When reporting suspicious activity over the VHF Radio, you should also take actions to protect yourself. If you are reporting on illegal or suspicious activity, keep in mind that the person or persons involved in the illicit activity may also be monitoring Channel 16. It is a good idea to cruise out of sight before using the radio to make a report. Being alert on the water will help our nation protect its borders.

Law Enforcement Authority

The U.S. Coast Guard and other marine officers can stop you.

A USCG boarding officer or other marine officer who observes a boat being operated in an UNSAFE CONDITION, specifically defined by law or regulation, and who determines that an ESPECIALLY HAZARDOUS CONDITION exists, may direct the operator to take immediate steps to correct the condition, including returning to port. Here are some examples of termination for unsafe use:

- Insufficient number of USCG Approved PFDs.

- Insufficient fire extinguishers.

- Overloading beyond manufacturer's recommended safe loading capacity.

- Improper navigation light display.

- Fuel leakage.

- Fuel in bilges.

An operator who refuses to terminate the unsafe use of a vessel can be cited for failure to comply with the directions of a USCG boarding officer or other marine officer, as well as for the specific violations that were the basis for the termination order. Violators may be fined not more than $1,000 or imprisoned not more than one year or both.

CHAPTER 4

BE PREPARED

Lines and Knots

What is a Line?

In boat terminology, rope is called line. Line is used for four principle purposes: pulling, holding, lifting or lowering. As a general rule, when a line is under stress, always keep an eye on it and NEVER stand where you can be injured in the event of an accident. Learning how to handle lines and tie knots can make a boating expedition more enjoyable, as well as safer. In making knots, you must know the parts of a line and certain basic turn patterns.

Knots

Knowing how to tie knots that both hold securely and can be undone quickly and easily is very important. You must be able to depend on the knots that you tie. Some knots are more suitable for particular purposes than others. This section gives a selection of the most common knots and their uses. Sailors have developed many types of knots over the centuries. This rope work, called Marlin Spike Seamanship, is a respected skill. However, the knots shown in this section can be used for most general purposes.

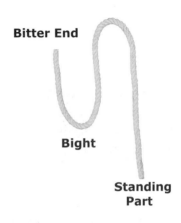

Bitter End

Bight

Standing Part

It is important when learning to tie knots that you understand the terminology used. The bend you make in the rope is known as the "bight", the part the bend is made over is known as the "standing part" and the end of the rope is the "bitter end".

Half Hitch

A half hitch is used to secure a line to objects such as a ring, piling or other structures. This knot is generally used to make a temporary fastening. One distinct advantage of this knot is that it can be quickly untied. The half hitch is the smallest and simplest hitch knot. Since a single half hitch may easily slip, it should not be used in situations where it will encounter great stress.

Two Half Hitches

To reinforce or strengthen the single half hitch, two half hitches may be used. This is a reliable knot to make the ends of a line fasten around its own "standing part". A boat can be moored to a piling or a rail using two half

hitches. When securing to a rail, it is important to tie the line near the rail's supporting blocks. This will prevent the line from slipping along the rail. Two half hitches in the same direction are referred to as "two half hitches".

Cleating A Line

Failing to cleat a line properly may cause it to slip or jam. The line should always be led (started) from the back of the cleat first, which will prevent it from jamming. You should take one full turn around the base of the cleat before making the figure eight turns.

Figure Eight

This knot is commonly placed at the end of a line to keep it from running through a block, cleat or other opening. One advantage of the figure eight is that it is easy to untie, even when wet.

Square Knot

A square knot is simple to make and is used for many applications for light duty work. This knot is made with a half hitch in one direction followed by another in the opposite direction. Typically, this knot is used to join the ends of two lines.

Bowline (b o-l — n)

A bowline is one of the most versatile knots. It can be used for a wide variety of purposes. The bowline will not slip or jam easily. It is the best knot to use for securing a heavy line to the end of a towline.

Safety Issues

Carbon Monoxide Poisoning

Carbon monoxide can be a "silent killer" on powered houseboats and other recreational vessels. Each year, boaters are injured or killed by carbon monoxide. Sadly, most of these accidental poisonings could have been prevented.

A NON-POWERED HOUSEBOAT

Photograph provided by Lyn Jewett

Carbon monoxide is a by-product of internal combustion engines. It is odorless, tasteless and very toxic, even in small amounts. Symptoms of carbon monoxide poisoning include eye irritation, weakness, dizziness, ringing in the ears, headache, nausea, loss of motion and unconsciousness. If anyone displays these symptoms, they should be moved into fresh air immediately. If the symptoms persist, you should seek medical assistance.

Carbon monoxide can collect within a boat in a variety of ways. Engine or generator exhaust leaks (the leading cause of death by carbon monoxide) can allow carbon monoxide to flow through the boat and into enclosed areas. To reduce the risk of carbon monoxide poisoning, make sure that your boat's generator is properly ventilated, keeping both the engine and generator exhausts clear. The best precaution against carbon monoxide poisoning is to keep air flowing through the vessel. You should also shut off your engine or generator when you are moored, anchored or not moving. Keep in mind that even properly vented exhaust can re-enter a boat, if it is moored too close to a dock or another boat, or if the exhaust is pushed back by prevailing winds. Under certain conditions, exhaust can re-enter boats, especially with canvas in place. Exhaust gases can also collect in enclosed spaces near the stern swim platform. You can prevent carbon monoxide poisoning by keeping your engine and generator well maintained as well as making sure your carbon monoxide detectors in the cabin are working properly.

Carbon monoxide poisoning can also occur outside your vessel. When in the water, avoid all areas near the engine exhaust. Inhaling engine exhaust and associated carbon monoxide may cause loss of consciousness and result in drowning. To avoid carbon monoxide poisoning, observe the following safety tips:

- Do not swim, sit near the swim platform or hold onto the swim platform when the engine is running ("Teak Surfing") or the vessel is underway.

- Do not moor next to another vessel whose engine is running.

- Be sure to recognize the signs and symptoms of carbon monoxide poisoning, not confusing them with seasickness or intoxication.

Man Overboard Guidelines

The majority of boating fatalities involving small boats are a result of persons falling overboard and drowning. To prevent falling overboard, both the boat operator and his or her passengers must take the appropriate precautions. Keep in mind that in a small boat, the weight of the passengers is often greater than the weight of the boat, causing a direct effect on the stability of the vessel. You should avoid sitting on the sides of a boat or any other part of the boat not designed for seating. Do not stand up when the vessel is moving. When you are stopped or moored in a small boat, only stand in the center of the boat and avoid leaning over.

Photograph provided by YMCA of South Palm Beach County, FL

Remember that even the best swimmers can become disoriented in the water after falling overboard. Immediate action is of primary importance when a "man overboard" situation takes place. Every second counts, particularly in heavy weather conditions. To save lives, every boat passenger should be aware of "man overboard" procedures.

Step One

The first person that recognizes that someone has fallen overboard should call out "MAN OVERBOARD!" and identify the side the person has fallen over, either the Starboard side or Port side. This person needs to maintain sight of the "man overboard" and continuously point to the person in the water. It is important for the people in the boat to refrain from rushing to the side of the boat the person fell over as this could cause small boats to capsize.

Step Two

Several events happen at the same time.

1. If the boat is equipped with LORAN or GPS equipment, the memory button should be set to mark the position where the incident occurred. Otherwise, turn the boat back in the direction the victim fell overboard. This will keep the stern of the boat away from the person in the water. Try to approach the person from downwind or by heading into the waves.

2. Another passenger throws a throwable flotation device (TFD), life saving device or floating cushion over the same side of the boat the person fell over. The floating device should be aimed upwind of the victim in the water so that it has a greater chance of blowing toward him. Use your knot skills and tie a bowline to the object being thrown to assist in pulling the person to the boat.

3. The passenger pointing to the "man overboard" goes to the bow, if weather permits, he continues to monitor the victim, and points to the location of the person at all times.

4. The captain makes preparations for the pickup.

5. The captain makes the recovery approach, briefing the other passengers on the boat as to how the recovery will be made and the side of the boat it will be made on. As you come alongside the person, the captain should turn off the engine or motor to minimize the risk of injury due to a propeller strike.

CHAPTER 4 – BE PREPARED

Step Three

Unless you are trained in saving a victim in the water, go for help. Victims in the water can be dangerous if you do not know how to properly handle the situation. Keep in mind the American Red Cross rescue sequence: **Reach, Throw, Row, Go**. First you try to **reach** the victim by using a pole, oar, shirt or similar device that can assist you in extending your reach to the victim. If there is nothing available that you can use to assist you in reaching the victim and the victim is close to the boat, lay flat on your stomach on the boat and offer your hand to pull the person to the boat. Be careful not to lean over the side of the boat and be pulled into the water yourself. If you cannot reach the victim using one of these methods, find a flotation device or other buoyant object, tie a line to it securing the end of the line to the vessel and **throw** the buoyant object to the victim in the water. Allow the victim to grab onto the buoyant object and haul him or her onboard at the stern of the vessel. If the victim is too far away for you to throw something to him or her and a non-powered boat is available, **row** to the victim and allow them to grab on to the stern of the boat. Do not try to haul the victim onboard since you can easily capsize your boat. Instead, row to shore with the victim hanging on to the boat. If the victim is unable to hang on to the boat, hold on to him or her until another person arrives to help. Only as a final option when all the other possibilities have been exhausted, should someone who is trained in lifesaving **go** into the water to retrieve the victim. Anyone who is not a trained rescue swimmer should go for help instead. If a rescuer does choose to swim to a victim, he or she should put on a PFD and carry a second buoyant object to give to the victim. If the victim is unconscious or injured, only a trained rescue swimmer should retrieve the victim. The rescuer should secure a line to a PFD and swim toward the victim, while another passenger holds the line attached to the rescuer's PFD. Once the rescuer reaches the victim, the passenger will then pull the line in with both the rescue swimmer and the victim.

Capsizing

Capsizing and falling overboard are the number one cause of boating accident fatalities. To minimize a capsizing accident caused by overloading a boat, refer to the portion of Chapter 3 that talks about the boat's capacity plate. If your boat capsizes, you should put on a Personal Flotation Device (PFD) or grab a Throwable Flotation Device (TFD). You should signal for assistance using visual distress signals, sound producing devices or a mirror. It is important that you do not try to swim ashore, but stay with the boat and the other passengers until help arrives. This is because most boats are equipped with flotation and are much easier for rescuers to spot in the water than a person or group of people. Only leave the boat as a last resort. You must focus on conserving your energy and body heat in order to prevent exhaustion and hypothermia. If possible, climb on top of the overturned boat. Reboarding the capsized vessel is especially important in cold water when keeping your body out of the water is essential. If you are unable to grab a flotation device or climb on top of the boat, grab another item that will help you float such as a cooler, oar or several empty soda bottles. You should also take a head count to make sure that everyone is present and accounted for. If there is a person in distress, follow the Red Cross Rescue Sequence: **Reach**, **Throw**, **Row**, **Go** discussed in the previous section.

Capsizing in a River

If you capsize in a river and are separated from your boat in a swift current, you should float on your back with your feet downstream. Do not try to stand up as your feet can be easily caught in rocks or trees on the river bottom as your body is forced downstream, possibly causing serious injury. Wait until you reach an area of the river where the current slackens and then try to either recover your boat or swim to shore if it is close enough for you to easily reach.

Cold Water Immersion

It is important to know that most man overboard victims that fall overboard in cold water do not die of hypothermia but of cold water immersion. Upon sudden immersion in cold water, the body's physiological shock response often results in death within the first five minutes, oftentimes long before the body feels the effects of hypothermia. Cold water immersion follows four stages including cold shock, swimming failure, hypothermia and post-rescue collapse.

Stage 1: Cold Shock

At the shock of hitting cold water, a body's natural reflex is to gasp. If a person's head is under water, his or her lungs can fill with up to two to three quarts of water. This is why it is important to have your PFD on prior to entering the water. If your lungs fill with this much water, you will not re-surface unless you are wearing a PFD. Following the initial gasp reflex, common responses include hyperventilation and rapid heart rate. Cold shock can also cause a heart attack. Generally, the cold shock stage lasts three to five minutes.

Stage 2: Swimming Failure

After the initial shock of hitting the water, victims will experience swimming failure after three to thirty minutes in the water. Swimming failure is a result of the rapid loss of manual dexterity and muscle control. This coordination loss causes the victim to assume a body angle that is incompatible with swimming and uses a greater amount of energy. Failure occurs when the victim is unable to make forward progress or keep his or her head above the water.

Stage 3: Hypothermia

While dependent on the water temperature, exposure, victim's clothing and other factors, hypothermia generally affects the victim after thirty minutes in the water. Hypothermia is discussed in greater detail in the next section.

Stage 4: Post-rescue Collapse

Even after rescue, a cold water immersion victim may still be in danger. As blood vessels in the victims' extremities re-warm, blood pressure can fall dangerously low. If the blood vessels fail to remain constricted, inhaled water can damage lung tissue. Heart problems can also develop as colder blood from the victim's extremities is released into the body's core. It is important to seek medical treatment for a cold water immersion victim as soon as possible.

Cold Water Survival

If an emergency occurs and you or one of your passengers falls overboard, there are some important points to remember while you are waiting to be rescued.

1. Know that wearing your PFD is imperative to surviving in cold water. A PFD will assist you in staying afloat, conserving energy and remaining visible to rescuers.

2. Do not panic. Try to control your breathing, taking slow breaths.

3. You must also attempt to keep your head and neck out of the water as you float. This is very important because about 50% of body heat loss is from the head. Do not attempt to remove any heavy clothing because air trapped in clothing can provide additional flotation.

4. Try to keep your movements to a minimum. Excess activity can cause you to lose your body heat quickly.

5. Maintain a heat conserving position by floating with your legs together, elbows close to your sides and arms folded across the front of your PFD. This position minimizes your body surface exposure to the cold water. If more than one person has fallen overboard, huddle together for warmth, facing each other with your arms around each other's shoulders.

6. If you cannot get into a boat, do not try to swim ashore. This will only decrease your chances of survival because swimming will cause blood to be pumped to extremities where it will cool more quickly.

7. Once you are in the boat, wrap yourself with clothing, life jackets and anything that you can find to cover your body, including your head, to help reduce body heat loss.

The U.S. Coast Guard has numerous documented cases where victims have been rescued with no apparent harmful effects after long immersions. If a person that has fallen overboard has been in the water for a considerable length of time and shows no signs of life, remember that it may be possible to revive him or her. If possible, start CPR immediately and get the victim to a hospital as quickly as possible.

Hypothermia

Hypothermia is a physical condition where the body loses heat faster than it can produce it thereby reducing the core body temperature. It is caused by exposure to wind, "cold" or wetness. The danger of hypothermia is greatest for a person immersed in cold water. Unlike cold-water immersion that can cause rapid death, hypothermia normally affects a victim after being immersed in water for a longer period of time. A common misconception regarding hypothermia is that a person is only at risk during very cold weather or if immersed in extremely cold water. In fact, hypothermia can affect anyone in conditions that are cooler than the body's core temperature. To prevent hypothermia, dress appropriately for the current weather conditions. If the weather is cold or windy, dressing in layers will help trap heat and keep you warm, even if you are suddenly immersed in water. Be sure that you are wearing clothing that protects areas of rapid heat loss such as the head, neck and groin. If you are going to be in the water during a boating activity, wear either a wet suit or a dry suit as necessary. Most importantly, wear your PFD and prepare yourself to suddenly be immersed in cold water.

The graph describes the average risk associated with immersion in water.

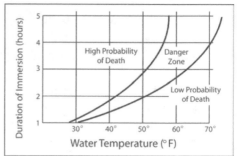

The Danger Zone indicates where safety precautions and appropriate behavior can increase your chance of survival when immersed in cold water. Follow the safety tips described in the previous section on Cold Water Immersion to increase your chance of survival during a "Falls Overboard" emergency. Symptoms of hypothermia include the following:

- Violent shivering

- Blue-gray lips, nail beds or skin color

- Muscle spasms

- Loss of feeling in or use of arms and legs

- Confusion or drunken behavior

- Dizziness

- Slurred speech

- Blurred vision

If left untreated, hypothermia can result in unconsciousness, a coma or death. A hypothermia victim should get medical treatment immediately; however, there are certain steps that you can take to help the victim. Get the person out of the wind, rain or water. Be gentle with the victim, restricting his or her movements. Do not allow him or her to walk unless absolutely necessary. Take precautions to warm the victim up slowly. Rapidly applying heat to a hypothermia victim can send the person into shock. Replace the victim's wet clothes with dry clothes. If he or she is conscious and alert, you can allow him or her to drink warm liquids that do not contain alcohol or caffeine. Cover the person in a blanket or any other material such as trash bags that will help his or her heat retention. If the victim is semi-conscious, keep the person awake. When you return to shore, seek medical attention as soon as possible.

CHAPTER 4 – BE PREPARED

Running Aground

Be familiar with your boat and shallow water locations to avoid running aground. By using a nautical chart, you can identify potential hazards such as sandbars or rocks that will be clearly marked on the chart. If you are operating in a body of water that is influenced by tides or currents, be sure to compensate for changes in water depth since some areas that are navigable in high tide are much too shallow at low tide to be safe. Should you run aground put on PFDs and check for damage to your vessel. If you are in a small boat, you may be able to step into the water and push yourself off. Check to make sure that your vessel is not taking on water, then shift your weight away from the point where the boat is grounded and push off using an oar or paddle. If you are operating a boat with an inboard/outboard engine, you should shift your weight away from the point of impact, stop the engine and lift the outdrive or propulsion unit. A larger boat may have to wait for high tide or be towed to deeper water. Waves and tidal action in some inlets can cause great damage to your boat and perhaps pose a safety hazard. If unable to free the boat, you should signal for help either visually or by using a VHF radio.

Checking Local Hazards

Nautical charts are very valuable when familiarizing yourself with a body of water. If the body of water has no available charts, use of "local knowledge" (local boaters, law enforcement officials and marina owners) can be invaluable to navigation, especially when confronting unmarked hazards like rapids, shoals or submerged cables as well as hazards that can potentially change from what is marked on the nautical chart, such as sandbars. Tidal tables can help navigation in an area with a tidal current and the National Oceanic and Atmospheric Administration (NOAA) weather channel broadcast on VHF radio can provide information about sudden changes in weather, including storms, heavy winds and hurricanes. When navigating unfamiliar waters, it is important to use as many "tools" as possible to ensure the safety of yourself, your passengers and your vessel.

Leeway

Be aware of the way your boat responds to wind and current. Both wind and current can cause boats to drift laterally or sideways when underway. This lateral or sideways movement is known as leeway. Wind will have a greater effect on a boat with a shallow draft while a boat with a deep draft and small cabin will be more affected by the current.

Dams, Locks and Bridges

A dam is built to restrict and control a body of water. Two types of dams that are hazardous to boaters are low head dams and conventional dams. Low head dams are constructed to provide small amounts of upstream water to another channel of water. They vary in height from one to several feet below the water's surface. The danger to boaters occurs when water flowing over the dam creates a strong circulating current at the base of the dam. Boaters can be trapped against the face of the dam and pulled under water even on small rivers. These dams pose a danger to boaters both above and below the dam. To ensure the safety of you and your passengers, do not go over or boat near a low head dam. The second type of hazardous dams is the conventional dams that have locks, powerhouses and spillways. These dams can easily be recognized as being dangerous to boaters and should be avoided.

Since dams control the flow of water from one body of water to another, at times water levels vary between these water bodies. Locks are then used as a means of controlling the water level. A lock is a section of waterway that can be closed on either end. Some locks are designed to allow boaters to pass through in order to safely travel between water bodies. When using a lock, always follow the lock attendant's instructions. Be aware that commercial traffic has the right of way over recreational vessels. When approaching the lock wait at least 400 feet away from the lock and signal the lock attendant using one prolonged blast to notify him of your intention to pass through. Do not proceed until the lock attendant allows you to do so. Once inside the lock have both line and fenders ready at hand to secure your vessel to the lock.

CHAPTER 4 – BE PREPARED

Bridges are other structures that can endanger boaters because they can obstruct visibility. Although many bridges are high enough for boaters to pass through, some may be drawbridges. If you have a boat that exceeds the clearance of a drawbridge, you must notify the bridge attendant by either signaling or radio of your intention to pass through. Always proceed with caution near bridges and operate at slow speed.

Prepare and Anticipate Weather

To prepare for a safe and fun-filled day of boating, you should make yourself aware of your weather, local water conditions, and your environment. In fact, you should make this a pre-requisite for planning your trip. Bad weather could ruin a day on the water, and in the worst-case scenario, become extremely hazardous. Before you leave land, you should get the weather information from the TV, radio, local newspaper, online or from one of the weather cannels on your VHF radio. Identify cloud formations because they can help you predict changing weather conditions.

Clouds

Cloud formations can help you predict changing weather conditions. Identify the cloud formations before you leave the dock and make it a point to check for cloud changes throughout the day. Two main types of clouds are stratus clouds and cumulus clouds. Stratus clouds form a horizontal base at lower altitudes when compared to cumulus clouds. These clouds look like a low gray blanket and normally bring some form of precipitation. Cumulus clouds are puffy

STRATUS CLOUDS

CUMULUS CLOUDS

in appearance with a flat base. These clouds usually mean fair weather, but can become thunderheads if they grow tall. A buildup of dark clouds is a common indicator of an approaching thunderstorm.

Storms

Conditions associated with storms such as increased winds, rain and lightning are often dangerous to boaters. At minimum, storms could delay your trip or cause an unpleasant end to your fun day of boating. In the worst-case scenario, storms could damage your boat or represent a life-threatening situation. If you are on the water and see an approaching storm, you should put on your PFD and head to the nearest safe port or marina.

Hurricanes

One type of severe storm is a hurricane. Hurricanes are tropical storms that form during the months of June through November and generally pose the greatest threat to the East and Gulf Coasts of the United States. Once a tropical storm strengthens to the point that its sustained winds reach 74 miles per hour, it is classified as a hurricane. Under no circumstances should boaters be on the water during a hurricane. Hurricane warnings are issued by weather services to alert boaters of a severe approaching storm. Once aware of the potential danger, boaters should not go out on the water until the danger has passed. Boaters should also take the proper precautions to ensure that their boats are stored and secured properly.

Wind

Changes in wind severity can be an indication of changing weather and sea state. Wind blowing over the water creates waves. If strong winds blow over the water for a long period of time, waves can build up to dangerous heights that threaten the safety of boaters. Sustained winds can also cause damage to rigging on sail boats, making it difficult to maneuver the boat. As with all dangerous weather conditions, boaters should head for shore when winds increase to avoid damage to their boat or potential injury.

Lightning

The most effective way to avoid a lightning strike is not to boat or fish in a thunderstorm. Before you leave the dock, prepare for a lightning strike by making sure your rigging is properly grounded, which will reduce the impact of the strike. When on the water, pay attention to worsening weather conditions by watching cloud formations and distant lightning. If conditions are deteriorating, quickly make your way to shore.

Fog

Fog is another dangerous weather condition that can negatively affect your boating outing. Fog can obscure your visibility and make it very difficult for you to navigate your boat. If you get caught in fog, make the required sound signals with your sounding device, navigate cautiously and head for shore.

Tides

Tides are the continuous rise and fall of the surface of bodies of water. The change from high to low tide usually occurs twice a day. To determine your local boating area's tidal flow, contact your local marina or U.S. Coast Guard station. Coastal states are greatly affected by tidal changes. Normal tide levels can fluctuate a few inches to several feet. The boat operator should be able to read and understand tide tables. It is important to understand tidal changes so that you can anchor and dock your boat.

CHAPTER 5

WATERWAY RULES

Disclaimer

The navigation rules of the road contained in this course summarize basic navigation rules for which a boat operator is responsible. Additional and more in-depth rules apply regarding various types of waterways and operation in relation to commercial vessels and other watercraft. It is the responsibility of a boat operator to know and follow all the navigation rules. For a complete listing of the navigation rules, refer to the document "Navigation Rules of the Road" published by the U.S. Coast Guard (COMDTINST 16672.2 Series) and available through the U.S. Government printing office or on the web at: http://www.uscg.mil/vtm/navrules/navrules.pdf. For state specific navigation requirements, refer to the state laws where you intend to boat.

CHAPTER 5 – WATERWAY RULES

Rules of the Road

As with other forms of transportation, there are rules you must follow when underway. These rules are called International Regulations for the Prevention of Collision at Sea, but for simplicity's sake they are often referred to as COLREGS, "the rules of the road" or "the rules of the water". The risk of a collision with another vessel became a major concern for captains when the second vessel was built and launched. Rules to prevent collision at sea were, historically, a fairly new idea. The first formal set of rules came into being around the middle of the nineteenth century (1850). These rules are divided into two classifications-Inland and International. In the majority of cases, the Inland and International rules regarding navigation are the same, but in some instances, they can vary. The Western Rivers system that includes the Mississippi River and its tributaries, and the Great Lakes System, including all of the Great Lakes and their tributaries may also have different rules pertaining to the safe operation of your vessel. Before operating your vessel, be sure to familiarize yourself with these rules. For a more detailed description of the waterways included within the Western Rivers and Great Lakes system, refer to the Glossary available in Appendix B.

It is important that every boat operator conducts his vessel in a prudent manner at a safe speed at all times. The operator should always maintain a proper lookout for other boats, swimmers or obstacles by all means available to him. A proper lookout includes using your sight, hearing and any other possible means such as a depth sounder or radar. In order to assist in communicating with another vessel, you will signal your intention to that vessel by using your sound-producing device (whistle, bell or horn).

"Give-way" and "Stand-on" Vessels

When you are within sight of another vessel while operating your boat, you must determine whether you are either the "Stand-on" or "Give-way" vessel, depending on your position. Your designation will either require you to take appropriate action to move out of the way of another vessel or to stay on your current course and speed.

Responsibility of "Stand-on" Vessels

If you are the "Stand-on" vessel you must continue on the same course and speed. If, however, it is apparent that the "Give-way" vessel is not taking the appropriate action to avoid a collision, you must maneuver your vessel as required to avoid causing or being involved in an accident.

Responsibility of "Give-way" Vessels

The "Give-way" vessel will surrender its course to the "Stand-on" vessel. As the "Give-way" vessel, it is your responsibility to alter your course as much as necessary to keep well clear from the other vessel.

Signaling Other Vessels

Your position as either a "Stand-on" or "Give-way" vessel and intention will determine the type of signal you must use to notify the other vessel. When you are near another vessel, sounding a whistle, bell or horn either once or twice with short blasts tells the other vessel the direction in which you plan to navigate your boat. To signal your intention of passing port-to-port sound one (1) short blast. If the operator of the other vessel understands the intention, one short (1) blast will be the reply. A "starboard-to-starboard" passage is only proper when there is no risk of collision or if special circumstances should exist. To signal the intention of passing starboard-to-starboard, you need to signal two (2) short blasts, if understood by the operator of the other vessel, two (2) short blasts will be the reply. The other vessel must repeat the same sounding signal you sent if he agrees or five (5) short blasts if he disagrees, doubts your intention or senses danger. These five (5) short blasts may be supplemented by five (5) short and rapid light signals. A short blast is a blast that lasts about one second. A prolonged blast is a blast that lasts four to six seconds. You must sound three (3) short blasts if your engine is in reverse. One (1) prolonged blast signals that you are leaving a slip.

CHAPTER 5 – WATERWAY RULES

Operating in a Narrow Channel

A boat, operating in a narrow channel, must keep as far to the starboard (right) side as possible. If you are operating a sailboat or a vessel less than twenty (20) meters in length, you should never prevent the operation of another vessel that can only navigate within a narrow section of the channel. You should never anchor in a narrow channel. When navigating a narrow channel, you should use appropriate sound signals and operate cautiously.

- If you are a motorboat caught in a fog, you should signal one (1) prolonged blast every two (2) minutes.

- If you are a sailboat caught in fog, you should signal one (1) prolonged blast plus two (2) short blasts every two (2) minutes.

Non-Motorized Vessels and Commercial Craft Situations

Any motorized boat must give way to the following vessels:

- Disabled boats or others that are not under command

- Boats that are performing tasks restricting their ability to maneuver such as boats maintaining navigational markers, performing underwater surveys or work such as laying cable or commercial fishing. This rule does not pertain to vessels engaged in fishing that are not restricted in their maneuverability such as fishing vessels using trolling lines.

- Any sailboat under sail unless it is overtaking.

Sailboats must also give way to the following vessels:

- Disabled boats or others that are not under command

- Boats that are performing tasks restricting their ability to maneuver such as boats maintaining navigational markers, performing underwater surveys or work such as laying cable or commercial fishing. This rule does not pertain to vessels engaged in fishing that are not restricted in their maneuverability such as fishing vessels using trolling lines.

It is especially important for vessels to stay clear of commercial craft. Due to the size of these vessels, they are normally constrained by their draft, meaning that due to the boat's draft in relation to depth and width of navigable water, these vessels are restricted in their ability to deviate from the course they are following and are restricted to operating in the channel. Also, they cannot slow down, stop or turn easily and are unable to see nearby boats. Because of these factors, commercial craft can present a danger to boaters. Boaters can best avoid this danger by avoiding operating near commercial craft.

Operating Under Sail

When two sailboats are approaching one another and are within sight of each other, different navigational rules apply. For the purposes of these rules, the windward side of the vessel can be easily recognized as the opposite side of the vessel that is carrying the mainsail. For example, if the mainsail is carried on the left (port) side of the vessel, then the right (starboard) side of the vessel is considered to be the windward side. In this example, the port side of the vessel is called the leeward side. When both sailboats have the wind coming over the same side of their vessel, the vessel to the windward is the "Give-way" vessel and must take the appropriate action to stay out of the way of the leeward vessel, the "Stand-on" vessel. When the sailboats have the wind coming over different sides of their vessel, the vessel with the wind coming over its port side must give-way to the other vessel. If a sailboat with the wind on its port side sees another vessel to its windward side but can not determine if the other vessel has the wind on its port or starboard side, it shall take every action necessary to keep out of the way of the other sailing vessel.

Collision Avoidance

Contrary to what you may think, most boating accidents occur during calm, clear weather with light winds. The navigation rules stipulate that all operators must use all possible means to avoid a potential collision. This includes maintaining a safe distance from all other vessels, allowing enough time to stop the vessel or maneuver to avoid a potential collision, operating the vessel in a prudent and responsible manner and signaling to indicate your intentions. You should consider your vessel at the risk of a collision if the compass bearing of another vessel does not appear to change and you are operating on converging courses. If you need more time to assess the situation and determine what action you should take in order to avoid a collision, slow your speed. Any actions taken to avoid a collision should be readily apparent to the other vessel observing either by radar or sight and made in ample time with due regard to good seamanship, allowing passing at a safe distance. Do not wait until the last minute to avoid another boat. Change course early enough to allow the safe passage of both the vessels. As a vessel operator, you must understand that the navigation rules do not exempt you from taking the necessary action to prevent a potential accident. A navigation rule can be overlooked if necessary to avoid immediate danger.

Restricted Visibility

While boating, you may find yourself in a restricted visibility situation, where the weather or conditions prevent you from seeing other boats, landmarks or navigational hazards in your area. Contrary to what you first may think, nighttime is not considered a low visibility situation. Examples of weather-induced reduced visibility include storms, fog, rain or haze. You can also face restricted visibility when navigating tight corners.

When you are operating your vessel after sunset or during periods of restricted visibility, you should turn on your navigation lights and operate at a safe speed considering the existing conditions. You must take actions to be aware of other boats in your vicinity, even if you are unable to see them. Pay attention to indications of nearby vessels such as other navigation lights, your radar or sounds of a horn or other sound-producing device. Be prepared for immediate action if you need to quickly change direction to avoid another vessel. If you observe another vessel on your radar screen and it appears there is a potential risk of collision, you must change your course as necessary to avoid the other vessel trying not to turn towards the other vessel when altering your course. If you hear the sound signal of another vessel, you must slow down to the minimum speed necessary for you to remain on course until you can determine the proper action to take in order to avoid the other vessel.

Boating Accidents

Similar to procedures followed during an automobile accident, a boat operator involved in an accident must give his/her name, address and vessel identification number to the injured person or owner of the  damaged property. Failure to report an accident or give identification is a state and federal crime and can result in fines or prison. The U.S. Coast Guard requires that accident reports be filed within 30 days of the incident when the accident involves loss of life, personal injury requiring medical treatment beyond first aid, property damage in excess of $2,000 or the complete loss of the boat.

Each state has different requirements regarding reportable accidents. Before boating, make sure to familiarize yourself with your state's laws addressing accident reporting. You can view an example of a general accident report form online at www.boater101.com. In addition, each state may have its own Boating Accident Report Form.

Rendering Assistance

It is unlawful for any person operating a vessel involved in a boating accident or any person that is a witness to a boating accident to leave the scene without giving all possible aid (to the extent they are able) to the involved persons as long as the assistance does not seriously endanger either the operator or the passengers of the aid-giving vessel. The Good Samaritan rules in the Federal Boat Safety Act of 1971 protect other boaters from liability if they render assistance in a reasonable and prudent manner.

Interference With Navigation

Except in the event of an emergency, it is unlawful for any person to anchor or operate a vessel in a manner that will unreasonably interfere with the navigation of other vessels.

Negligent Operation

The law prohibits negligent or grossly negligent operation of a vessel and/or interference with the safe operation of a vessel, so as to endanger lives and/or property. The U.S. Coast Guard may impose a civil penalty for negligent operation. Grossly negligent operation is a criminal offense and an operator may be fined up to $5,000, imprisoned for one year, or both. The following are some examples of actions that may constitute negligent or grossly negligent operation:

- Operating a boat in a swimming area.

- Operating a boat while under the influence of alcohol or drugs.

- Excessive speed in the vicinity of other boats or in dangerous waters.

- Hazardous water skiing practices.

- Bow riding, also riding on seatback, gunwale or transom.

The most frequent example of negligent operation is operating a boat with excessive speed. While the term excessive speed immediately brings to mind a boat flying across the water throwing a large wake, it also means a speed that is excessive for the area where you are operating. Increased vigilance in maintaining an appropriate speed must be used in congested areas, fog or stormy conditions. Pay attention to your surroundings and avoid cutting through and disrupting a marine event such as a regatta or marine parade in progress or operating near a dam. If you are towing a water skier or a person on some other aquaplaning device, you must not operate your vessel in a manner that would cause the towed person to run into another vessel or structure or be hit by another vessel. When no limits are posted, the boat should be operated in a manner that will not endanger other vessels. Courtesy also dictates that you slow down when passing near swimming areas, fishing boats, marinas or other possible navigation hazards. Remember, you are responsible for any damage caused by your wake. The maximum speed for boats within 200 feet of a swimming beach, diving platform or passenger landing is five (5) miles per hour. You must also slow to five (5) miles per hour within 100 feet of a swimmer.

Common Navigational Situations

The three most frequently encountered navigational situations are Head-On, Crossing and Overtaking. These situations will be discussed in further detail in the next section. It is important to note that, in navigational situations, all boats that are not propelled by engine power, such as sailboats, canoes, and rowboats, have right of way over motorboats unless it is a situation described previously, in which they must give way to disabled boats or boats restricted in their maneuverability.

Head-On

There are six points that you should remember about Head-On Situations:

1. When vessels meet "head-to-head", both are "Give-way" vessels. There is NO "Stand-on" vessel. If you are involved in this type of traffic situation at night, you will see both sidelights and the masthead light of the other vessel.

2. Consider an approaching vessel "nearly ahead" if the vessel is within one point (11 1/4 degrees) on either side of the bow.

3. If there is any doubt as to whether you are in a head-on situation, assume you are and act accordingly (sound maneuvering signals and maneuver to keep clear).

4. It is the duty of each vessel to pass "port-to-port" sounding appropriate maneuvering signals while they remain in sight of one another. To signal your intention of passing port-to-port sound one (1) short blast. If the operator of the other vessel understands the intention, one short (1) blast will be the reply.

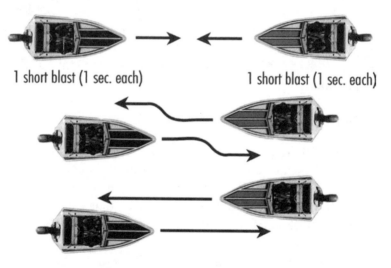

1 short blast (1 sec. each)   1 short blast (1 sec. each)

HEAD ON: PASSING PORT TO PORT

5. A "starboard-to-starboard" passage is only proper when there is no risk of collision or if special circumstances should exist. To signal the intention of passing starboard-to-starboard, you need to signal two (2) short blasts, if understood by the operator of the other vessel, two (2) short blasts will be the reply.

6. The doubt or danger signal, 5 short and rapid blasts, shall be sounded when a vessel fails to understand the intention of another vessel or doubts sufficient action is being taken to avoid collision by another vessel.

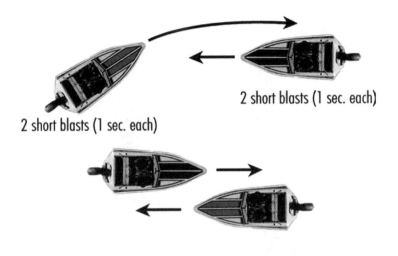

2 short blasts (1 sec. each)

2 short blasts (1 sec. each)

HEAD ON: PASSING STARBOARD TO STARBOARD

Overtaking

An overtaking vessel is defined as a vessel that is passing a second vessel, starting from the stern 22.5 degrees behind the beam of the vessel being overtaken and moving forward past the second vessel. Another way to describe it is if the overtaking vessel is in a position to stern of the second vessel where at night the vessel operator would only be able to see the stern light but not either of the side lights. In this situation, the overtaking vessel is the "Give-way" vessel and must stay out of the way of the vessel being overtaken, the "Stand-on" vessel. The "Give-way" vessel sounds two (2) short blasts to pass the "Stand-on" vessel on its port side. The "Stand-on" vessel should maintain its speed and course. The "Give-way" vessel sounds one (1) short blast if it wants to pass the "Stand-on" vessel on its starboard side.

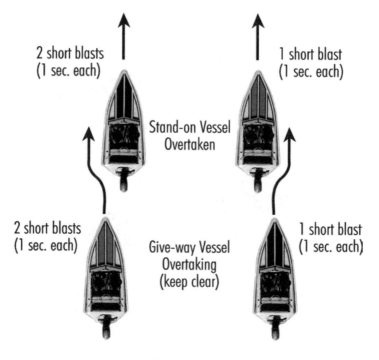

2 short blasts
(1 sec. each)

1 short blast
(1 sec. each)

Stand-on Vessel
Overtaken

2 short blasts
(1 sec. each)

Give-way Vessel
Overtaking
(keep clear)

1 short blast
(1 sec. each)

OVERTAKING

Crossing

When vessels are within sight of each other (with risk of collision) and are not meeting "head-on" or in an "overtaking" situation, you are considered a crossing situation. At night, you will see either the red or green sidelight of the other vessel.

If you see the port side of another vessel, stop because the other vessel has the right of way. You are the "Give-way" vessel and must change your course. When you alter your course, you should cross to the stern of the other vessel. You should avoid crossing ahead of other vessels under normal circumstances. If at night you see a starboard (green) light, you are "Stand-on"; if you see a Port (red) light, you are "Give-way". The "Give-way" vessel must take early and substantial action to stay out of the way of the other vessel ("Stand-on"). In a crossing situation, if you operating a powerboat and are the "Stand-on" vessel and the "Give-way" vessel is not altering its course sufficiently to avoid a collision and you are required to alter your course, you should avoid altering your course to the left (port) if the "Give-way" vessel is on your port side.

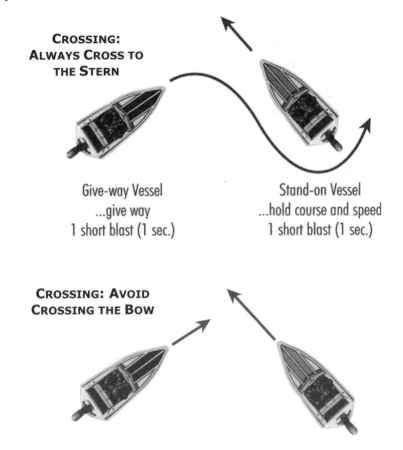

**CROSSING:
ALWAYS CROSS TO
THE STERN**

Give-way Vessel
...give way
1 short blast (1 sec.)

Stand-on Vessel
...hold course and speed
1 short blast (1 sec.)

**CROSSING: AVOID
CROSSING THE BOW**

Western Rivers and Great Lakes System

If you are operating a powerboat on the Great Lakes or Western Rivers System, the vessel proceeding in a downstream direction has the right-of-way over a vessel traveling in an upstream direction. In this instance, the vessel traveling downstream is the "Stand-on" vessel and the vessel traveling upstream is the "Give-way" vessel. When crossing any of these bodies of water in a powerboat, you are the "Give-way" vessel and must stay out of the way of vessels traveling in both an upstream and downstream direction. If you are operating a powerboat on a narrow channel within these systems and are the "Stand-on" vessel traveling downstream, you will indicate the manner and location of passage, signaling your intentions to the "Give-way" vessel and taking the necessary actions to allow safe passage.

Anchoring Your Boat

The most important rule to remember when anchoring is that you should NEVER anchor by the stern. Anchoring from the stern has caused many small boats to capsize and sink. The transom is usually squared off and has less freeboard than the bow. In a current, the force of the water can pull the stern under. The boat is also vulnerable to swamping by wave action. Since you may need to use your anchor in an emergency situation, you should keep your anchor in a readily accessible location, where it can be reached quickly. Do not store it underneath other equipment or in an area that is difficult to reach.

The key to successful anchoring lies in dropping the anchor at the right moment. Here are some general steps to follow in proper anchoring:

- Direct the bow of your boat into the wind or current and put your engine in neutral.

- As the boat begins to drift back from the anchoring site, slowly lower the anchor from the bow to the bottom by hand using the anchor line.

- After you have lowered the anchor, check to see that it is holding securely by backing down on the anchor. Place the engine in idle and then reverse to help set the anchor.

- As a general rule the anchor line should be seven to ten times the depth of the water plus the distance from the water to where the anchor will attach to the bow. A three to six foot length of galvanized chain should be attached to increase the holding power of the anchor and to hold up to abrasion.

- Keep hold of the anchor line until you have secured it to the boat.

- To prevent a boat from capsizing or taking on water never anchor from the stern.

- Make sure you have the right anchor type for the depth of water and type of bottom where you are boating.

Docking and Mooring

There are a number of factors that affect your vessel when docking or mooring. You need to be aware of these as a boat operator so that you can safely dock and moor your vessel. When docking, you must first consider the size of your boat. Be sure to choose a location that leaves you plenty of room to maneuver your vessel comfortably. If you are inexperienced in docking, practice docking in an uncongested area where there are few other boats. Second, you must consider the type of boat that you have and its maneuverability. For example, boats with displacement hulls will handle differently than planing hulls when docking. Third, consider where you are trying to dock. Mooring at a face dock requires different maneuvers than entering a slip. Fourth, you must also consider the effect of wind and tidal current when a boat is leaving or arriving at a dock. Fifth, you must consider boat traffic in your docking area. Be sure to keep a 360-degree look out at all times while docking to avoid an accident or a potential dangerous situation. There are no rules to help you decide which method of leaving and returning to use. You must learn to apply your knowledge of your boat and the experience you have gradually built up to work out the best solution. Also remember, when turning, that the stern of the boat swings in the opposite direction from which you are turning.

Approaching the Dock

When approaching a dock, the main objective is to stop the boat in the right position. Be prepared to have fenders in place and lines ready. Be ready to use forward, neutral and reverse gears. In the absence of a tidal current, this usually means approaching head-to-wind, using the wind to stop the boat. Where present, a tidal current will often have more of an effect on the boat than the wind, so docking into the current is better.

Docking without wind or tidal current

Approach the dock bow first, at a 10- to 20-degree angle. Have your bow line ready. As the bow nears the dock, use your reverse gear to slow down your forward movement. When mooring your boat in this situation, first secure the bowline, then the stern line.

Docking with wind and tidal current from the dock to the water

Approach the dock bow-first at a sharper angle than you would normally. Moor your boat by tying up the bow, and use your engine power to swing the stern to the dock.

SHARP APPROACH ANGLE

Docking with wind and tidal current from the water to the dock

Make your approach parallel to the dock. Use the wind and tidal current to move you to the dock. Moor your boat to the dock with your lines.

PARALLEL APPROACH

Docking into the wind and tidal current

Slow your speed, and at a shallow angle approach the dock either down wind or down current. You can put your engine in reverse to maintain your position. When mooring, your stern line will be the first line you tie up.

SLOW SPEED AND SHALLOW ANGLE

Leaving the Dock

The tidal current normally runs parallel to a wall, dock or pier, but the wind could be blowing from any direction. When you are leaving a dock, use your bow and stern line to help pivot the boat so that either the bow or stern points away from the dock. This prevents the boat from rubbing alongside the dock as you

LEAVING THE DOCK

try to leave. You should, however, start your engine with the mooring lines tied to the dock. You do not want to be adrift without steering power in a congested area. Whether you leave bow or stern first depends primarily on the position of the boat in relation to the direction of the wind or tide.

Boating Under the Influence

Every boater needs to understand the dangers of boating under the influence of alcohol or drugs (BUI). The use of alcohol contributes to approximately one-third

of all boating accidents. Research by the U.S. Coast Guard (USCG) indicates that in over half the deaths resulting from alcohol-related boating accidents, victims capsized their boat or were lost overboard. Boaters can avoid these dangers by boating safely with a designated boat operator if they are planning on drinking while on the water.

Because of the danger an impaired operator poses to himself, his passengers and other boaters, BUI became a specific federal offense on January 13, 1988. Also, all states have their own legislation prohibiting BUI.

CHAPTER 5 – WATERWAY RULES

1. It is a violation of federal and state law to operate a vessel while impaired by alcohol or other drugs. A vessel operator suspected of boating under the influence must submit to sobriety tests and a physical or chemical test to determine blood or breath alcohol content (BAC).

2. Federal law states that a vessel operator is presumed to be under the influence if their blood or breath alcohol level is at or above 0.08% for operators of recreational vessels being used only for pleasure. Individual states may have different blood or breath alcohol levels.

3. Any person under 21 years of age who is found to have a breath alcohol level of 0.02% and operates or is in actual physical control of a vessel is in violation of federal laws.

The Effects of Alcohol

Alcohol decreases reaction time, impairs motor functions and judgment, and blurs vision. These are all dangerous side effects for boaters, who must rely on these functions constantly while on the water. It is also important for boaters to recognize that alcohol can impair a boater much faster than a person on land. A drinker's impairment is accelerated by factors that cause fatigue. Factors associated with boating including motion, vibration, engine noise, sun, wind and spray can increase the effects of alcohol and rapidly impair the boater. Boaters who are legally of age to drink must be aware of these effects to ensure their safety on the water.

CHAPTER 6

ENVIRONMENTAL PROTECTION

Aquatic Nuisance Species (ANS)

The spread of invasive species, also known as Aquatic Nuisance Species by recreational boaters, is an increasing concern across the country. Invasive species often compete with native species causing damage to the natural resource and depleting fish stocks. Milfoil, zebra mussels and other ANS are being increasingly regulated by states to prevent their spread, with specific regional, state and local laws. You should be aware of your state laws concerning ANS and do everything you can to help prevent the spread of ANS by observing the following procedures:

- Clean all mud and aquatic plants from your boat, motor and trailer before leaving the boat ramp at a waterway.

- Drain your boat by emptying your live well and bilge before transporting it to a new boating location.

- Use a mild bleach and water combination to disinfect your boat.

- If possible, allow your boat to completely dry for at least twenty-four (24) hours before transporting it to a new boating location.

Disposal of Toxic Substances

Oil Pollution

BOOM DEPLOYMENT

Both state and federal laws prohibit boaters from releasing oil or hazardous materials into or upon the navigable waters of the United States. The United States Federal Water Pollution Control Act stipulates that vessels 26 feet in length and over must display a placard at least five by eight inches, made of durable material, fixed in a conspicuous place in the machinery spaces, or at the bilge pump control station stating the following:

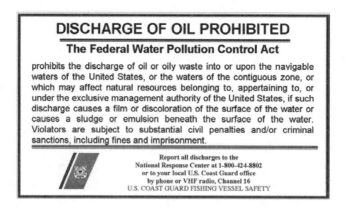

DISCHARGE OF OIL PROHIBITED

The Federal Water Pollution Control Act

prohibits the discharge of oil or oily waste into or upon the navigable waters of the United States, or the waters of the contiguous zone, or which may affect natural resources belonging to, appertaining to, or under the exclusive management authority of the United States, if such discharge causes a film or discoloration of the surface of the water or causes a sludge or emulsion beneath the surface of the water. Violators are subject to substantial civil penalties and/or criminal sanctions, including fines and imprisonment.

Report all discharges to the
National Response Center at 1-800-424-8802
or to your local U.S. Coast Guard office
by phone or VHF radio, Channel 16
U.S. COAST GUARD FISHING VESSEL SAFETY

Any release of this type of material will cause sheen upon the water that can be damaging to the environment. All boats with engines that use gasoline, diesel or an oil and gasoline mixture to operate should carry oil and fuel absorption equipment. In the event of a discharge, the used absorption material must be properly disposed of on land. One of the areas on a boat that is the most susceptible to trapping oil and fuel products is the bilge area. The bilge area is located in the lowest part of the boat's hull and collects water and other liquids. When the liquids in the bilge area reach a certain height, a float switch activates

SPILL CONTAINMENT

a bilge pump, which pumps the liquid overboard. If the bilge pump does not work, the boat could fill up with water and sink. Due to the close proximity to the engine area, bilge liquids can easily become contaminated with products leaking from the engine. Like routine maintenance performed on automobile engines to prevent grease and oil from leaking onto the ground, boat engines must also be regularly maintained to prevent oil, grease and petroleum products from leaking into bilges.

In the event that sheen is observed on the bilge water, do not pump the water overboard. Absorption material should be placed in the bilge area to capture the floating product before the water is pumped overboard. This material, which is sold in both sponge and solid forms, should be stowed safely until you reach shore at which point it should be discarded in compliance with local and state laws. No person may intentionally drain oil or oily waste from any source into the bilge of any boat. Non-compliance with these regulations results in severe fines and penalties being administered by the state. By taking the proper precautions through engine maintenance and the use of absorption materials in bilges, we can ensure that our waterways remain free of pollutants.

SEA OTTER COVERED IN OIL

The fuel that powers our voyage can cause pollution

If it is possible, try to fuel away from the water. Fuel and oils, also known as petroleum products, can cause pollution to the environment if not handled properly. Petroleum products contain hydrocarbons, and in some cases heavy metals, which are poisonous to aquatic life even in very small quantities. Petroleum products float on the top of the water and even the smallest drop will spread quickly when spilled into the water, especially when a strong wind or tidal current is present. It is also important that you follow the proper fueling instructions described in Chapter 3 in order to ensure that fuel does not leak into your bilge.

Cleaning Products

It is also important for boaters to be aware that many cleaning products used on boats have additives that are toxic to the environment. Protect your waterways by using all of the cleaning product rather than dumping extra product overboard. Make sure that you are using the cleaning product for the proper use by reading the directions on the label. Save empty containers and properly dispose of them on land rather than throwing them overboard. Individual states may have different regulations concerning proper disposal of cleaning products including fines for non-compliance. Be sure to check with your applicable state agency to ensure you are following the appropriate laws.

Proper Garbage Disposal

The Refuse Act of 1899 prohibits the throwing, discharging or depositing of any refuse matter of any kind (including human waste, garbage, oil and other liquid pollutants) into the waters of the United States. It is illegal to dump garbage into navigable waters of the United States. In addition the Act to Prevent Pollution from Ships (MARPOL ANNEX V) places limitations on the discharge of garbage from vessels. Types of garbage prohibited include: plastic, rope, floating material, food waste, paper, rags, glass, metal and bottles.

Garbage Type	Discharge
Plastics - including synthetic ropes, fishing nets and plastic bags	Prohibited in all areas
Floating dunnage, lining and packing materials	Prohibited less than 25 miles from nearest land
Food waste, paper, rags, glass, metal, bottles, crockery and similar refuse	Prohibited less than 12 miles from nearest land
Comminuted or ground food waste, paper rags, glass, etc.	Prohibited less than 3 miles from nearest land

CHAPTER 6 – ENVIRONMENTAL PROTECTION

United States boats 26 feet or longer must display in a prominent location, a durable *Garbage Disposal* placard at least four by nine inches notifying the crew and passengers of the discharge restrictions. Oceangoing vessels of 40 feet or longer, which are engaged in commerce or are equipped with a galley and berthing area, must have a written Waste Management Plan describing the procedures for collecting, processing, storing and discharging garbage, and designating a person in charge of carrying out the plan.

Although the dumping of garbage is prohibited, trash often accumulates on beaches and at the shorelines of waterways. As a proactive response to this type of pollution, many state marine trade associations sponsor Waterway Cleanups. The Cleanup brings people together to pick up the trash discarded in our waterways. These items pose a hazard to the aquatic environment and will remain in the environment for many years unless picked up by caring individuals.

Discarded items such as those listed below will sometimes even release chemicals that are harmful to living creatures. Garbage can also cause other types of problems. For example, birds eat cigarette butts, plastic pellets and polystyrene foam pieces, and they can be entangled in fishing line. To prevent endangering our waterways and aquatic wildlife, never throw your trash overboard. Except for what you consumed, always bring back to shore everything that you took aboard. Individual states may have different regulations concerning proper garbage disposal. Be sure to check with your applicable state agency to ensure you are following the appropriate laws.

Degradation Rates

Item	Rate
Aluminum can	200-500 years
Plastic 6-pack ring	450 years
Cotton rag	1-5 months
Plastic bottle	Over 500 years
Cotton rope	3-14 months
Wool sock	1 year
Paper bag	2-4 weeks

Proper Waste Disposal

Human waste should not be dumped into the water. Boats that are equipped with marine toilets or heads must have a system to manage their sewage. Federal law states that dumping untreated sewage, even if it has been treated with a deodorant product, into any inland waters or the water within three (3) miles from shore along the Pacific and Atlantic coasts, within nine (9) miles of the shore along the Gulf of Mexico or navigable rivers is illegal and can cause serious health consequences.

According to the U.S. Coast Guard (USCG), boaters have three options to assist them in treating their waste. These options are referred to as Marine Sanitation Devices (MSDs). MSDs are devices attached to marine toilets that either treat the raw sewage to an affluent level acceptable discharge or contains the raw sewage until it can be pumped out at a sewage pump out facility.

1. A Type I MSD today uses several technologies that breaks waste matter down to destroy all harmful bacteria. Some actually kill viruses and use no harsh chemical additives.

2. A Type II MSD also breaks down waste but to a finer degree and disinfects waste as well. These devices are for bigger boats over 65 ft.

3. A Type III MSD is generally described as a "Holding Tank".

When you are using a Type I or II MSD, you must make sure that when discharging your treated sewage, you are doing so in a legal manner. In addition to the federal regulations regarding appropriate release of treated sewage, states often have areas denoted as no-discharge zones where it is illegal to release any type of sewage, treated or otherwise. Be sure to check with your local authority before discharging in order to ensure that you are following the state's regulations.

Boaters who use USCG approved Type III holding tanks are encouraged to use pump outs and not bypass the holding tank. If you have a holding tank that is equipped with a "Y" valve, it must be secured in the closed position by using a padlock, non-releasable wire tie or removing the valve handle whenever you are operating your vessel in U.S. waters. To encourage boaters to avoid dumping sewage offshore, Congress passed the Clean Vessel Act in 1992. This Act established a federal grant program to increase the number of available pump-out and portable toilet dump stations as an alternative to overboard disposal of recreational boater sewage. As a result, all recreational vessels must have access to pump-out stations funded under the Clean Vessel Act. Check your nautical charts for the pump-out location nearest you.

Preserving our coastal water quality is essential to maintaining a healthy thriving aquatic ecosystem. Raw or poorly treated sewage can spread disease, contaminate shellfish and lower oxygen concentrations in the water. Using Marine Sanitation Devices and pump out facilities contributes to a cleaner, safer environment for our boating enjoyment.

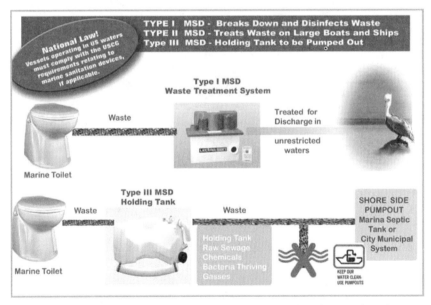

Graphic provided by Dale and Dawn Weatherstone of Raritan Engineering

STATE REGULATIONS

Each state has boating laws in addition to the federal regulations discussed in the previous chapters that are unique. You must familiarize yourself with your state's regulations to ensure that you are following all the appropriate laws. These laws are available for download from the Boater101 web site: www.boater101.com. A practice exam may also be available online depending on your state's mandatory boating education requirements.

GLOSSARY

Aboard   On a boat

Aft   In or near the stern of a boat

Aground   When a boat hull is touching bottom

Amidship   In or toward the center of the boat

Anchor   A casting shaped to grip the sea bottom and hold a boat in place by an attached rope

Aquaplaning Device   Any type of device that you can use to skim on the surface of the water, i.e. boat, water skis, jet skis

Astern   Toward the stern of a boat

Backfire Flame Arrestor   A device attached to an engine's carburetor that prevents a fire from leaving the carburetor system in the event of a backfire; required for all gasoline engines

Beam   Width of a boat at its widest point

Bilge   The internal part of a boat's hull

Biodegradable   Capable of being broken down into harmless products

Bow   Forward or front part of a boat

Can Buoy   Green, white or black, cylindrical buoys with odd numbers that are positioned on the left side of channels when returning from sea

Capacity Plate   A placard required on all boats; lists the maximum weight capacity for the boat as well as the horsepower rating

GLOSSARY

Capsize   To tip over

Catamaran   A boat with two hulls that are connected by a deck

Chart   A map that shows the characteristics of a body of water; includes navigational aids, hazards to navigation such as reefs or shoals and water depths

Deep Vee Bottom Hull   A hull design that is in the shape of a "V". These hulls plane well and through the addition of an engine with greater horsepower, can produce a comfortable ride

Displacement Hull   A hull designed to move water out of the way as it plows through it

Draft   The vertical depth measured on a boat from the waterline to the lowest part of the hull

Flat Bottom Hull   A stable type of hull design but provides a bumpy ride when operated at high speeds

Float Plan   A form to be submitted to a local authority or relative on land before leaving port; includes a description of the boat, people onboard, radio equipment, trip plan, and emergency notifications

Forward   Moving towards the bow of a boat

Freeboard   The vertical distance measured on a boat from the waterline to top of the transom

Give-way Vessel   The boat that must take immediate and significant action to avoid colliding with another vessel when following the Rules of the Road (see "Stand-on" Vessel)

Great Lakes System   Includes the Great Lakes and their connecting and tributary waters including the Calumet River as far as the Thomas J. O'Brien Lock and Controlling Works (between mile 326 and 327), the Chicago River as far as the east side of the Ashland Avenue Bridge (between mile 321 and 322), and the Saint Lawrence River as far east as the lower exit of Saint Lambert Lock

Gunwale   The upper edge of a boat's side

Head   A marine toilet

Helm   The steering wheel controlling the rudder of the boat

Hull   The body of a boat

Hypothermia   A physical condition where the human body loses heat faster than it can be produced

Idle Speed   The minimum speed that is necessary to maintain steerage of your vessel

Intracoastal Waterway (ICW)   The ICW is a toll free waterway that is 3,000 miles long. It stretches along the Atlantic Coast from Boston, MA to Key West, FL and along the Gulf of Mexico coast from Apalachee Bay, FL to Brownsville, TX

Knot   A unit of speed on the water that is equal to one nautical mile (6,076.10 feet) an hour

Leeward   Located on the side away from the wind (See Windward)

Line   General term for rope on a boat

Line of Demarcation   Marks the dividing point between inland and offshore waters

Livery   A boat rental facility

Log   A record of a boat's journey

Manually Propelled Vessel   Any vessel that is not mechanically powered by an engine (i.e. canoes, sailboats under sail, kayaks, rafts and rowboats)

Mooring   A permanent anchor or buoy that a boat can attach to while in one location

GLOSSARY

Motorized Vessel   Any vessel that is mechanically powered by an engine.

Multihull   Having one or more hulls; provides more stability and less resistance when moving through the water

Nautical Mile   Equal to 6,076.10 feet; longer than a standard mile

Navigable Bodies of Water   Waterways that are directly connected to the ocean, so are therefore affected by tides and are capable of being navigated by vessels for the purpose of reaching the ocean

Negligent Operation   The operation of a vessel and/or interference with the safe operation of a vessel, so as to endanger lives and/or property

No Discharge Zones   Waterway zones in which neither treated nor untreated sewage may be released into the water

No-Wake Speed   See Idle Speed

Non-Motorized Vessel   Any vessel that is not mechanically powered by an engine (i.e. canoes, sailboats under sail, kayaks, rafts and rowboats)

Nun Buoy   Red buoys with even numbers that are positioned on the right side of channels when returning from sea

Oar   A long paddle used to propel a boat forward

Onboard   On the boat

Outdrive   The propulsion unit on an inboard/outboard or stern drive engine.

Planing Hull   A hull designed to lift out of the water at high speeds

Port   1) The left side of the boat as you face forward 2) A destination or harbor, i.e. when a boat is docked it is in a port

Powerboat   Any vessel that is mechanically powered by an engine

Rigging   A general term for all of the lines on a boat

Round Bottom Hull   A hull designed to be easily maneuverable but may tip easily

Rudder   The device by which a boat is steered

Sailboat   Vessels that are being operated by sail only. Since many sailboats are equipped with engines, they are considered powerboats when they are in use, even if their sails are up

Spar Buoy   A channel marker that narrows at the top from a round base; used to replace any other type of buoy

Stand-on Vessel   The boat that must continue on the same course and speed when following the Rules of the Road (See Give-way Vessel)

Starboard   The right side of the boat as you face forward

Stern   The rear or back of the boat

Swamp   To fill with water

Throttle   A mechanical part of the boat that regulates the speed of the engine

Tide   The rise and fall of waters controlled by the gravitational pull of the moon and sun

Transom   The outside of a boat's stern

Underway   When a boat is in motion

GLOSSARY

Vee Bottom Hull   A hull designed to provide a smooth ride in choppy waters

Wake   The path left by a moving boat in water, a wave

Waterline   The line where the hull intersects with the water when a boat is fully equipped for operations

Western Rivers System   Includes the Mississippi River, its tributaries, South Pass, and Southwest Pass, to the navigational demarcation lines dividing the high seas from harbors, rivers, and other inland waters of the United States, and the Port Allen-Morgan City Alternate Route, and that part of the Atchafalaya River above its junction with the Port Allen-Morgan City Alternate Route including the Old River and the Red River

Windward   The side of the boat towards the wind (See Leeward)

INDEX

INDEX

INDEX

INDEX

Boat Operations Checklist

<u>Each Trip</u>

☐ Make sure all exhaust clamps are in place and secure

☐ Look for exhaust leaking from the exhaust system components evidenced by rust and /or black streaking, water leaks, or corroded or cracked fittings.

☐ Inspect rubber exhaust hoses for burned or cracked sections. All rubber hoses should be pliable and free of kinks.

☐ Confirm that cooling water flows from the exhaust outlet when the engines and generator are started.

☐ Listen for any change in exhaust sound that could indicate a failure of an exhaust component.

☐ Test the operation of each carbon monoxide detector by pressing the test button.

Do not operate the vessel if any of these problems exist!

<u>At Least Annually:</u> (Performed by a qualified marine technician)

☐ Replace exhaust hoses if any evidence of cracking, charring or deterioration is found.

☐ Inspect each water pump impeller and inspect the condition of the water pump housing. Replace if worn or cracked (refer to the engine and generator manuals for further information).

☐ Inspect each of the metallic exhaust components for cracking, rusting, leaking or looseness. Pay particular attention to the cylinder head, exhaust manifold, and water injection elbow.

☐ Clean, inspect and confirm the proper operation of the generator cooling water anti-siphon valve (if equipped).

Float Plan

1. Boat Operator/Description of the Boat
   a. Operator Name/Telephone Number:

   _____

   b. Boat Registration Number/Name:

   _____

   c. Make/Size:_____

   d. Fuel Capacity: _____

   e. Number of Engines:_____

2. Number of Persons Onboard:____
   Name/Address_____

   _____

   Name/Address_____

   _____

   Name/Address_____

   _____

   Name/Address_____

   _____

3. Radio Equipment
   a. Type:_____

   b. Call Sign:_____

   c. Cell Phone:_____

4. Trip Plan
   Leaving From:_____

   Going To:_____

   Departing On (Date and Time):_____

   Returning On (Date and Time):_____

5. If not returned by:_____
   Notify:_____

6. If emergency arises call: _____
   a. Coast Guard_____

   b. Local Authority_____

Pre-Departure Checklist

Before leaving the dock, be sure that you take a few minutes to complete the following checklist.

Minimum Federal Required Equipment
- [ ] State Registration Documentation
- [ ] State Numbering Displayed
- [ ] Certificate of Documentation
- [ ] Life jackets (PFDs) – one for each person
- [ ] Throwable PFD
- [ ] Visual Distress Signals
- [ ] Fire Extinguishers (fully charged)
- [ ] Proper Ventilation
- [ ] Backfire Flame Arrestor
- [ ] Sound Producing Device(s)
- [ ] Navigation lights
- [ ] Oil Pollution Placard
- [ ] Garbage Placard
- [ ] Marine Sanitation Device
- [ ] Navigation Rules
- [ ] Any Additional State Requirements

Recommended Equipment
- [ ] VHF Marine Radio
- [ ] Anchor and Tackle
- [ ] Chart(s) of Area & Navigation Tools
- [ ] Magnetic Compass
- [ ] Fenders and Boat Hook
- [ ] Mooring Lines and Heaving line
- [ ] Manual Bilge Pump or Bailing Device
- [ ] Tool Kit
- [ ] Spare Parts (fuses, spark plugs, belts)
- [ ] Spare Battery (fully charged)
- [ ] Spare Propeller
- [ ] Extra Fuel & Oil
- [ ] Alternate Propulsion (paddles/oar)
- [ ] Flashlight & batteries
- [ ] Search Light
- [ ] First Aid Kit
- [ ] Sunscreen (SPF 30+)
- [ ] Mirror
- [ ] Food and Water
- [ ] Extra Clothing
- [ ] AM – FM Radio
- [ ] Cellular Phone
- [ ] Binoculars

Safety Checks and Tests

- [ ] Test VHF Marine Radio (voice call)
- [ ] Test Navigation and Anchor Lights
- [ ] Test Steering (free movement)
- [ ] Test Tilt/Trim
- [ ] Test Bilge Pump
- [ ] Check for any excessive water in bilges
- [ ] Check Fuel System for any leaks
- [ ] Check Engine Fluids
- [ ] Ensure Boat Plug is properly installed
- [ ] Check Electrical System
- [ ] Check Galley/Heating Systems
- [ ] Check gauges (i.e. Battery)
- [ ] Check Fuel Amount
- [ ] Ensure Anchor is ready for use
- [ ] Check load of vessel and secure gear from shifting
- [ ] Ensure passengers know Emergency Procedures and Equipment Location
- [ ] Everyone put on a life jacket to check for proper fitting
- [ ] Check the Weather Forecast
- [ ] File a Float Plan with family or friend